MASQUES OF
MORALITY

MASQUES OF MORALITY
Females in Fiction

by

JOHAN LYALL AITKEN

The
Women's
·Press·

For Helen Rosamond
Jenifer Eelin and
Joanne Frances

and in memory of
Margaret Laurence

CANADIAN CATALOGUING IN PUBLICATION DATA

Aitken, Johan Lyall, 1933-
Masques of morality

Bibliography: p.
ISBN 0-88961-113-0

1. Women in literature. 2. English fiction –
History and criticism. 3. Canadian fiction –
History and criticism. 4. American fiction –
History and criticism. I. Title.

PN56.W6A58 1987   823'.009'352042   C87-093906-8

Cover Art: "Compassion," sculpture in bronze
by Almuth Lutkenhaus,
photographed by Arthur Lackey

This book was produced by
the collective effort of members of
The Women's Press

Printed and Bound in Canada

Published by
The Women's Press
#204-229 College Street
Toronto, Ontario M5T 1R4

CONTENTS

ACKNOWLEDGMENTS

In Alexander Pope's phrase, I am "indebted to no prince or peer alive," nor to any foundation, grant or agency. I am, however, deeply indebted to the many texts and contexts of which I have been privileged to partake. I will resist the segregation of helpers — secretarial, medical, personal, domestic, academic. Such distinctions blur: I am forever hearing the words from one arena of my life echoing in all the others. I wish to thank my family, my teachers, my friends, my students, my colleagues and in particular Don Aitken, Clive Beck, Alan Brown, Ken Butler, Jan Drysdale, Doris Dyke, Northrop Frye, Robin Harris, Sandy Healy, Peggy Hill, Beverley Kirkland, Markus Koenen, Liz Martin, Sonia Melkonian, Joan Scott, Alan Teachman, Joanne Thompson and Charis Wahl. I should add that my recent inclusion in the lunch bunch provided the necessary momentum to cross the finish line and that the help of Michael Sinelnikoff has made all the difference.

Manners and morals are so nearly allied that they have often been confounded; but although the former should only be the material reflection of the latter, yet when various causes have produced factitious and corrupt manners which are very early caught, morality becomes an empty name.

Mary Wollstonecroft

The novel is the best way to think through each strenuous moral struggle in the explicit detail which it deserves.

Fred Inglis

If women's stories are not told, the depth of women's souls will not be known.

Carol Christ

▲

Preface

Is it a girl or a boy?
   "The most important thing to know about a person in our society is its sex."[1]

I suspect that my present interest in females in fiction began when I was a young child. I come from a long line of readers and have read, or been read to, all my life. Being an only child, I peopled my world with characters from my stories and usually assigned myself a central role. Flopsy, Mopsy and Cottontail could have all the berries and cream they liked: I could never be anyone but Peter! For weeks I was David the shepherd boy, marching my toy sheep up and down the green carpets of a gabled third-storey room. A harmonica, or mouth organ, as we called them then, served me well as a harp. Having no brothers with whom to be compared, I may have enjoyed this happy state of being anyone I liked for longer than most girls: I certainly had more uninterrupted pretending time. However, I well remember the day I realized that I could be Miriam but not Moses, not because of my age — that would never have bothered me — but because I was *just* a girl. I couldn't lead anyone anywhere, let alone to the Promised Land.

Hope for the future does not die in the young, so I began my search in stories and in poems for females I could not only pretend to be, but whom I would also *like* to be. When I began to study English, I quickly adopted what Jane Miller calls *learned androgyny*, a way of thinking that allows us as readers to enter into stories that exclude us, for example *Moby Dick*. Miller explains why feminist criticism strikes some women as narrow, since it requires them to see male characters as *other*. Miller urges women readers to "relearn androgyny...to sensitize them to exclusionary situations in life."[2]

I now recognize that I was consciously preparing for this book when, to my male professor's consternation, I first wrote in 1960 about the *representation* of women in the nineteenth-century novel. Since that time, at least, I have included among my various readings of all texts — print, film or theatre — a decidedly female approach. In the past decade, particularly, I have been aided in this enterprise by the impressive rise in audibility of feminist criticism. Reader curiosity has been heightened and intensified as to how story-tellers, seers and artists describe and narrate females.

Readers are also more aware of what is known as "intertextuality" — the ways in which a number of different texts operate within an apparently single text. We are also increasingly alert to the effect of texts upon each other. In fact all the texts we have ever known are present whenever we read. Writing and reading are increasingly thought of in concert, and as social, rather than exclusively solitary, pursuits. For example, the man who dedicates his novel to his wife "without whom this book could never have been written" may speak the whole truth, however unconsciously: she may well have been his unrecognized collaborator. Similarly, we often take in ideas and rhythms from other texts through our pores as we read. We would be at a loss to explain these sources as they reappear, only partially transformed, in what we innocently refer to as our very own work. Texts influence one another in their genesis and development. They also speak to one another through time and space. Recognizing these phenomena has helped contemporary readers to make conscious connections among texts, and between these texts and their own lives. Does art really hold the mirror up to life, or do we more often become what we behold?

In *Masques of Morality* we explore what goes on in the lives of twenty-five females in fiction. Through an individual character, whose environment and personality we come to know, we may learn more about the realities of various societies and "woman's place" in those societies than we would from endless charts and statistics. What are the uneasy tensions between appearance and manners on the one hand, and feelings and morality on the other? We tend to behave as we are expected to by our group or organization. Many of the fictional females we consider dislike these expectations, but bend to them nonetheless. Others reject them; still others try to change the expectations themselves. Individual females, of course, perceive their societies in many combinations of engagement and detachment. We may not agree with their perceptions, but we can usually understand them. The political exploitation of females, both subtle and overt, is a thread that runs through all our stories. Art makes it possible for us to experience how closely aligned the seemingly separate worlds of the personal and the political may really be. We are forced to question the extent to which any woman has self-determination. In reading, in experiencing females who are animals, children and women in many times and places, we are partially freed from the blinkers of our own space and culture. "Texts are places where power and weakness become visible and discussable, where learning and ignorance manifest themselves, where the structures that enable and constrain our thoughts and actions become palpable."[3] Through our many masques, then, we have some chance of knowing ourselves, or of being known. Through an understanding of stories, we begin to perceive the influences of socialization, politics and aesthetics that have shaped our consciousness of who we are and, more often, of who we are not. By looking at our cultural images past and present, we may be not only empowered to choose, but enabled to change.

Literature is more than a thwarted investigator; it is also an incorrigible perpetrator of the problem of sexuality: literature *pre*scribes thought and action according to the dictates of certain ideologies just as surely as it *de*scribes them. There are primary concerns, such as "life is better than death, freedom better than slavery, happiness better than misery." There are also secondary concerns, "what we call ideology, the desire of a particular social group, or a class or priesthood or bureaucracy or other special interest within that group, to preserve its ascendancy or increase its prestige. Every work of literature, as something produced for its own time, is an ideological document."[4] One of the ways in which we will consider texts is as ideological documents. Every reader has an ideology and nothing is more blinding than an assumption that is not known to be one. In writer, in text, in critic, in reader reside matching and conflicting ideologies, which this book explores as masques — the narrative about our lives and about what we call "life" that we spin together, tell each other and repeat in a multiplicity of versions.

Long before the expression *role model* was coined, girls and women aped the thoughts, speech and behaviour of the heroines of fiction. That codes of manners and systems of morality have dictated thought and action to both sexes in all times and places is self-evident. That more restraints have been placed upon females is undeniable. Common to most societies, past and present, moreover, are economic and social forms of dominance and submission that may, as many theorists insist, spring from the dominance and submission of the sexual paradigm. Such connection can be effectively considered through the real lives of women in fiction.

▲

This book is divided into six chapters. Chapter One, **Who Cares About the Text?**, provides a philosophical and theoretical overview. Literary theory has never before been so popular. Esoteric journals and literary studies have no monopoly on post-structural and feminist theories. The professions, the social sciences and virtually all studies in the arts and culture are making use of their insights and techniques. As always, the more we know about the foundation and framework of our literature and language the better grounded our explorations will be. The study of semiotics — of words and the magic of naming — can enlighten: we need the ammunition that this analysis of language provides if we are to make any sense of the tangled language web that might ensnare us. Textual power needs careful scrutiny to be transformed into personal power: Chapter One attempts to provide a basis for this activity.

The order of the chapters that follow is one that I observed taking shape as I read and wrote. The material might well have fallen within different contours instead of into these five overflowing groups. Yet a distinct philosophical stance buttresses not only the stories I have chosen for each group but indeed all the books, plays and films I have experienced in fifty years. Within each division there is great variety, but the characters belong together because of their positions, their dilemmas, their attitudes or their actions.

I have chosen stories that, at some time in my life, have been important to me and to many other women. I believe that it is essential to see texts in their own contexts. We should not blame eighteenth-century writers, for example, for not having our view of the cosmos, of nature or, for that matter, of sex roles. I have tried to understand why women in fiction, whatever their time and place, think and act as they do. I am interested in the moral framework that surrounds them, and their individual morality within it. That our personal and social relationship with texts may have little to do with indexes on some powerful literary stock exchange has become increasingly obvious to me. Some of my choices have the blessing of the academy; others do not. By juxtaposing stories we are not accustomed to seeing on the same lists, I have tried to show that my story list, like anyone's, is idiosyncratic and nonconformist. Nobody can write anyone else's canon. The stories, the plays, the films to which we return as to a well to quench our thirst tell a great deal about who we are. Thus, there is always some risk in the sharing of texts, particularly if one goes against the grain in one's choices. It is this risk, free from value judgement, that I encourage the reader to take.

Chapter Two, **What Is To Be Done?**, begins with Jane Austen's *Emma* and groups females who, like Emma, find the limitations imposed by their time and place difficult to accept. In every case the main character has a lively imagination and thinks of some way to overcome or get round her plight. These are not females who sit down and opine on their fate or status, nor do they knuckle under and accept the way things are. Rather they stress the need to *do* something. This attitude brings together females who take seriously the question, What is to be done? This is the common denominator of Emma and an eighteenth-century prostitute, a female rabbit from the country, an old black woman in the United States and a young girl growing up in Toronto during the Great Depression. Females in fiction fit into this category of irrepressible planning and action.

Chapter Three, **Can Anything Be Done?**, tells in a great variety of forms the oft-repeated hopelessness of the lives of many women — hopeless simply because they are female. In a world of patriarchy they are habitual victims. They do not seek to be martyrs; they do not want to be victims. *Tess of the D'Urbervilles* by Thomas Hardy, the opening story, moves inexorably through a catch-22 situation to the death of a beautiful woman. All the while the reader asks," Is this necessary? Can anything be done?" In this chapter, too, a contemporary upper middle-class white woman is trapped by her allegiance to the rules of society's game, a mother and her daughter have their lives maimed because of a father's neglect and a society's indifference, a woman in Puritan New England must suffer public condemnation and another in Quebec has no real choices and no permanent escape from her role as female victim. In spite of their diverse backgrounds, I see these suffering, isolated women bound together. When we see that the suffering imposed upon such women is the result of misogynist factors built into socio-economic and belief systems, it is small wonder we despair.

Chapter Four, **Grace Under Pressure**, is the most ambiguous. Try as I might, I could not fit the girls and women of this section, and the countless fictional females they typify, into any other category. I admire these characters: they are spirited, and possess high intelligence and considerable moral strength. None is strictly conventional within her own context, yet none, in the end, defies the system completely and risks upsetting the social order. The first novel in this group is *Portrait of a Lady* by Henry James. The tale ends with Isabel, the central figure, exhibiting grace by remaining in a cruel mockery of marriage. Grace shows itself under a variety of pressures: taking in stride without resentment or bitterness the disappointments and changes of childhood, being the loving wife and nourishing mother to one's children and to an extended, unrelated family, deciding to be an artist and not to marry in spite of social censure, freeing a much-loved husband without rancour or blame so that he may marry again, and relinquishing a scholarship to stay home with an ageing guardian. All these females have a deep and unswerving sense of commitment, of a kind that may not enjoy widespread popularity today. Nevertheless, all those who show such grace need to be seen against the backdrop of their individual worlds — and to be recognized. They represent countless women whose choices and decisions are complex and whose touchstone is grace.

In Chapter Five, **Rebellion Under Pressure**, I have grouped stories about girls and women who have the courage of their convictions: they are all appealing characters, capable of fighting for good reasons, including that of becoming themselves. The first character we meet is Morag Gunn, the central presence of Margaret Laurence's novel, *The Diviners*. At every stage of her life she must rebel in order to grow and move on. The more I thought about Morag, the more I found she had affinities with a host of characters whom I love. Regardless of when their stories were first told or written, they have a timelessness about them and an affinity with much of what is currently being written about females by females. I found it difficult to choose among the many tales of rebellion under pressure, and the reader may wish to add many more to the appendix. These females have strong wills; they hang on; they overcome. Among those who belong with Morag we find a girl who shoves an old witch into the oven, and another, computer-wise in a multicultural society, who, when she must fight, fights fair. Two American civil-war heroines — one from the north and one from the south — prove their independence and resourcefulness as they rebel against the roles prescribed for women in their cultures. All these rebels with causes and the sisterhood to which they belong reveal strong personalities clashing with unfriendly circumstances and carrying the day.

In Chapter Six, **Towards a New Mythos**, we move through pain and longing to discover what happens when one refuses to be a victim, when one decides not only to rebel against the system but to change the rules. The first story is that of Rose, the hero of Alice Munro's *Who Do You Think You Are?* Rose is unwilling to become what she beholds in the lives of girls and women around her. What she, and anyone wishing to force paradigms to shift, must do is blaze new trails. Two kinds of stories seem to belong in this group: one that shows someone caught in the midst of rapidly changing value systems, and another that depicts heroes who discover that a new mythos is needed, and who help, by the choices they make and the chances they take, to bring it into being. Both sorts of stories abound, and they were not all written in the last lap of the twentieth century. An English mom, who has no other identity, shows us that, however painful the birth pangs of a new mythos, its arrival is sorely needed. A shaggy little dog who leaves hearth and home helps us on our way. A wild girl from a folk tale shows us that female quest and adventure are possible, and a hero with no name proves that in our time such lives may no longer be exceptions but may lead to a genuinely new understanding of what females can do and be.

Masques of Morality concludes with an appendix of additional texts, listed according to category, and a list of related readings. While current theory brings into serious question the distinctions traditionally made among texts, for purposes of convenient retrieval, this list is divided into Literary Criticism: general; Literary Criticism: feminist; and finally, Feminist thought regarding language and semiotics.

There remain three matters that I should mention at the outset: the sex of the authors, the Canadian writer and children's literature.

Ethical leaders of influence have traditionally told stories, capturing the imagination and presenting human paradigms and models. These stories have had an overwhelming impact upon human thought and action. Most leaders, however, have been male, and quests, journeys and adventures have been undertaken largely by men or heroes. The hero may have had a thousand faces but the genitalia have remained the same. Feminist theorists agree that the female in life and in fiction must be released into full humanity. However, they do not agree on whether this release will cause the bright expansion of the language and structures of a tradition already in place or whether we must build an entirely new edifice that will admit light and air to replace the musty and suffocating structures imposed upon women by patriarchy.

Because evolution rather than revolution may still be possible, and because the oppressed may enjoy the spoils of the oppressors, I have opted for portrayals of women by women and men writers. It may well be true that, as Annette Kolodny observes, men cannot fathom the female experience: "The male critic, only recently exposed (if at all) to women's language (written or otherwise), could not possibly begin to analyse it adequately; the best of our women critics and scholars will hardly be adequate to the enormous task — but at least they will begin from a necessarily more informed base."[5]

Novels written by men have, until recently, however, shaped the consciousness and guided the behaviour of both women and men. We get nowhere denying the way we were. Rather than indulging our pessimism about the limits of the human imagination, we can look forward tentatively to a time when we may come of age, producing artists who are simply and splendidly human. Such a time may never come. Women may find that they must go it alone, in literature and in all the arts. Separation would be unfortunate if for no other reason than that it would give men another excuse not to read the writing of women, which has power to enlighten and enable them. Our current theories of literary influence also need to be tested in terms of women's writings. If a man's text, as Bloemard Edward Said has maintained, is fathered, then a woman's text is not only mothered but parented; it confronts both paternal and maternal precursors and must deal with the problems and advantages of both lines of inheritance.

In my selection of texts, and in my choice of critics and theorists, I have been guided in the main by two criteria. In the case of the stories, the female character — her resources and conflicts — has been my major concern. As the manners, morals and motives of women in fiction were of paramount importance, and as I had decided against the male habit of exclusivity, Thomas Hardy, and Henry James suggested themselves. When their protagonists have justified it, other male writers have been included. As Nina Auerbach has noted: "In accepting too obediently the tenet that men mutilate their heroines to suit their own myopic needs...feminist criticism may indeed be mutilative to the women whose lives it wants to expand. For in excluding male visions from its canon, it may also be dismissing a faith in growth, freedom and fun, of which women's worlds, in literature at any rate, are in general sadly deprived."[6]

A feminist reading of a great deal of criticism written by men will find much that irks and offends and, worse still, much that would perpetuate our dependence upon male modes of thought. It is becoming clear that a methodology of our own is needed and, indeed, may already be ours. Thus far, feminist criticism has concentrated upon content; method, the more elusive twin, is often glossed over or ignored. Sometimes, of course, as in criticism of Virginia Woolf's *Three Guineas*, fear of content is masked by an undue concern for method. (Those who most condemn Woolf's organization and method are scared to death of her content.) In an effort to repress content it is still easy to hide behind the gods of traditional literary criticism — logical progression, beginnings, middles and ends, consistency of voice, separation of subject and object, and a dependence upon the *correct* sources. However, women are developing not only a content of our own, and a voice of our own, but also a method of our own. Because it is impossible to define does not mean such a method does not exist. (We have long been at home with entities that defy precise definitions.) For example, the world of closure, the false sense of being "finished" is an environment alien to most of us.

> Ending is difficult for Woolf. She tells us in *A Writer's Diary* that the more one's vision encompasses, "the less it is able to sum up and make linear."...she deliberately subverts the linearity of history by juxtaposing it to the circularity of poetic imagination....Woolf undertakes the task of revising linear determination by complicating it through an understanding of woman that is nonexclusive, bridging the extraordinary and the ordinary woman.[7]

Careful deconstruction of female critical method is necessary if we are to get hold of our own methodology and put it to work. We may find that the methodology conceived by the female imagination is every bit as significant as the content.

It was satisfying to note how many of the works chosen for the nature of their heroines were by Canadian authors. Rosemary Sullivan suggests that:

> It is possible that the status of being a colony — as women are often described — within the Canadian colony has given a particular emphasis to women writers in this country. As a writer in a colonial context, where the writing of literature was itself a presumptuous art, women could claim equal authority with their male colleagues....Even for the modern Canadian writer, cultural identity remains an issue. Once the writer focuses on the confusions over national identity, colonialism can, paradoxically, be turned into a source of strength — the writer discovers a new sense of cultural responsibility: to define a people to itself. The circles of identity — personal, cultural — conflate.[8]

Canadian literature is world-class literature — it is a good thing *and* our own — taking its place alongside fiction originating in other countries. We are not provincial, exclusive or chauvinistic; women in Canadian fiction can enjoy their well-earned place in the sun.

Finally, we come to what is commonly called children's literature. If a system is theoretically sound, its basic principles can be taught to young children. It is in very early childhood that the notion of who we are — our identity, as we call it — begins to develop. Probably at no stage in our life-long learning is the influence of story so potent. Literature read to and by children is, most emphatically, literature. In a book lamenting the position of women in life and in fiction, a book celebrating the casting off of stereotypes, it would be sadly ironic if the exclusivity adopted by men towards women were extended by women to children. Children's masques are serious business. Their play, like our own, is built out of and builds back into the stories we relate and read to ourselves and each other. Tony and Tatterhood help us to formulate and to tell our own tales. There are not really "children's issues" or "children's content" but human issues and human content. Children feel frightened, alone and incapable; so do adults. Just as adults desperately need the lively presence of the young in their midst, so literature and the study of the female in fiction is incomplete without tales enhanced by the young.

Adults frequently underestimate children's ability to hear and read through the words to the meaning. We have often defined readability as if style, morals and aesthetics were not really important; yet genuine readability includes all these elements. Finally, it is frequently through an examination of literature loved by children that we first see clearly the masques that define the sex roles we have been taught to play. Sometimes merely by locating an early influence we can determine its usefulness. Incorporating valued elements from once-loved texts into a new system of thought may well serve us better than casting these stories from us, even if this were possible. The important thing is to exercise our right to pick and choose. Children's literature may also, of course, be the place in which we meet the new mythos of the liberated female hero and recognize her for the first time. Chronological snobbery, however, will get us nowhere. Some of our ancient tales possess the seeds of a new mythos. As Jane Marcus implies in *Thinking Back Through Our Mothers*,[9] these old stories are a rich resource, and strong females reach around the world and across the centuries to help us and to urge us on.

Feminist critical theory has taught me not to be afraid or ashamed of my responses to texts; it has freed me to admit that there are some "great" books I shall never read again and some that enjoy little official recognition to which I long to return. Having outlined the genesis of *Masques of Morality*, the criteria for selecting its texts, its organization, resource materials and several of its peculiarities, I hope the reader will take whatever she finds useful from the chapters that follow, adding, revising and producing a new text as she goes.

▲

CHAPTER ONE

WHO CARES ABOUT THE TEXT?

IN CONTEMPORARY LITERARY THEORY, the text — that objective, self-contained art object of yesteryear — has come under attack. We now admit that print cannot catch meaning and fix it for all time. Each generation of readers, each special-interest group and perhaps each and every reader will read a different version of *Anna Karenina* or *Mary Poppins*. Think, for example, of the range of responses — agreement, laughter, curiosity, disdain, cynicism, to name a few — that might be provoked by the opening sentence of *Pride and Prejudice*: "It is a truth universally acknowledged, that a single man in possession of a good fortune, must be in want of a wife."[1] Such a disarmingly "simple" sentence can lead to endless speculation: there is nothing simple about its possible meanings. We have always known that different readings of scripture could give rise to different belief systems but we have been slow to recognize that a wide variety of *readings* could be expected from readers engaged in reading and interpreting any text.

In schools and universities there has been considerable stress on toeing the line, on accepting what the greats said about the Greats (the canon of obligatory texts for a scholar and a gentleman). This was not a bad way to begin, but the club was too exclusive and the self-confidence of the student to think independently often undermined. The more convinced, and convincing, students were in their adherence to the accepted creed — usually that of New Criticism — the better they were likely to fare in the system. This is not to say that there have not always been teachers as well as students who were mavericks and rebels, who had ideas of their own, voiced these ideas and encouraged others to do likewise. Some of us owe our very survival to the influence and support of just such imaginative teachers. Since literary theory thrives on controversy, there was always sufficient disagreement among the "authorities" to ensure that some individuals would begin to trust their own responses and evaluations. Now, with the advent of what contemporary theorists call "deconstruction"*, the hardy individual has become the accepted norm. The apparently unassailable text has been displaced by the interpretive community, and the lionized author by the all-powerful reader. This change in emphasis and in belief in where meaning resides has altered almost everything. The individual reader has been freed to read, but with that freedom has come the responsibility of discerning and producing meaning. As each reader brings to a text an enormous number of assumptions, biases, concerns and experiences (of both life and literature), a new confusion reigns. In addition, a new language for talking about texts has arisen. Deconstruction encourages us to open up texts, to ask entirely new questions about them. Meaning is found or caught in the interplay of what we call signifiers. Meaning, it is held, consists in difference — cat is only cat because it is different from rat or eat, because it is different from *all* other words. Words and phrases in a context remind us of other words and phrases that are alike but also different. As well, they remind us of themselves in other contexts. These traces are always present in any reading act: a large, if not infinite, number of *traces* may be unleashed by any

---

* "Derrida's celebrated 'deconstructions' of ... writings in which he brings to light the internal contradiction in seemingly perfectly coherent systems of thought, constitute a powerful attack on ordinary notions of authorship, identity and selfhood since they are a demonstration that, even when it is being used most consciously, language has powers we cannot control. Derrida himself exploits the alarming 'productivity' of language to destabilize existing philosophical systems."
Sturrock, *Structuralism and Since* (Oxford: Oxford University Press, 1979), p.14.

(For a comprehensive explication of the theory of deconstruction, see "Related Readings".)

word or group of words. Deconstruction challenges the alleged distinctions between writing and reading and between literary and non literary texts; it reveals how arbitrary and insubstantial such distinctions may really be. In our deliberations, the aspects of deconstruction that can serve us best are those identified by Gayatri Spivak:

> The recognition, within deconstructive practice, of provisional and intractable starting points in any investigative effort; its disclosure of complicities where a will to knowledge would create oppositions; its insistence that in disclosing complicities the critic as subject is herself complicit with the object of her critique; its emphasis upon "history" and upon the ethico-political as the "trace" of the complicity; the proof that we do not inhabit a clearly defined critical space free of such traces; and, finally, the acknowledgement that its own discourse can never be adequate to its example.[2]

This succinct and inclusive list is one to which the reader may wish to return, for it lays out our strength, insight and power when we deconstruct a text. It also reminds us of our limitations; our complicity with all we do; the importance of *trace* in all reading and writing; and finally of the limitations of discourse itself.

Women have quite regularly appeared in texts and, under male names or their own, have even written a good number of them; but until very recently criticism has been the province of men and the male point of view has predominated. The 1952 edition of W.J. Bate's *Criticism: The Major Texts*, a ubiquitous university textbook, gives the impression that no female literary theorists of consequence exist. The 1970 "enlarged edition" is, as one would expect, more comprehensive and up-to-date: it includes Northrop Frye, Thomas Mann and Jean Paul Sartre. Among the fifty-three critics allowed within these hallowed pages of "Lit Crit," however, the only female is Virginia Woolf.* She may be

---

*In William Ray's *Literary Meaning: From Phenomenology to Deconstruction* (1984), another much-studied text, there is no mention of feminist criticism *or* Virginia Woolf in the index, let alone the table-of-contents. The "authorities" are taken seriously — and they are all male!

the mother of us all in feminist criticism but her solo appearance at a time when not only feminist literary theory but female literary critics abound indicates that the scholarly establishment still considers the female voice an aberration. Feminist theory is included in such widely used texts as Terry Eagleton's iconoclastic *An Introduction to Literary Theory*; yet the female feminist literary critic, with her prolific and revolutionary writing, is inconspicuous or invisible in the critical mainstream.

Feminist criticism, dependent as it was for its early impetus upon deconstruction, is more than an offshoot or subspecialty of deconstruction. It is also more than an aberration in understanding life and literature and their symbiotic relation. The concept of différence freed women to value their own perceptions and voices; however, it caught us in another bind. We can reverse the value assigned to each polarity and refer to "women and men" rather than "men and women," but, as many feminists have noted, it still leaves man as the determining referent, not departing from the opposition male-female but participating in it. Feminism is less inclined to polarize, to believe in binary opposition than other forms of deconstruction: many perspectives can be tolerated with relative ease within a feminist framework. In fact, it is to feminist thought that we owe the ability to deal with difference without constituting an opposition.

It is essential that feminist theory break loose from its dependence upon Great White Fathers. Much of what has passed for feminist criticism is entitled *Marx and Feminism*, *Derrida and Feminism*, *Lacan and Feminism*, and, perhaps most tiresomely, *Freud and Feminism*, as if the very existence of feminist critical theory depended upon its juxtaposition in a linguistically secondary position to what we revealingly call a "seminal" male thinker. Whenever men have written in ways that open possibilities for women, their work will be useful to feminist reading and interpretation. We need, however, to rid ourselves of the notion of *master thinker* of either sex. Master thinkers are always in danger of controlling, limiting or closing off genuine criticism; authority of this kind stems from male dominance that purports to have the only answer. Literary theory is now in desperate need of profound questions and of readers who, by pushing texts almost to the breaking point, risk asking those questions. If we are to outgrow the paradigm of dominance and submission, master and slave in literary deconstruction, we must first outgrow demagoguery. As Hélène Cixous warns, however,

> Great care must be taken in working on feminine writing not to get trapped by names; to be signed with a woman's name doesn't necessarily make a piece of writing feminine. It could quite well be masculine writing, and conversely, the fact that a piece of writing is signed with a man's name does not exclude femininity. It's rare, but you can sometimes find femininity in writings signed by men: it does happen.*[3]

It will not help in the long run to replace male demagogues with female ones; it is not sufficient to disrupt a hierarchy, if people simply exchange positions in the order.

It is virtually impossible, however, to overestimate the difficulties of making an impact upon prevailing ideology, committed as it is, in its theory and institutions, to patriarchy. We have learned our lessons in hierarchy well and effectively, not only through societal structures but also through stories and carefully controlled interpretations of those stories. By concentrating upon the position and depiction of women in the written text and in the context of their lives in the world, we can see that life and literature shed light upon each other: life imitates art just as surely as the other way round. We can focus upon morality and politics; we can refuse to shy away from their uncomfortable arenas. The ethical component, the "moral of the story," will not disappear in some bright white light of pure aesthetic theory, for nothing women or men have ever written is uncontaminated by ideology or untainted by systems of morality.

All texts are biased — and mine is no exception. I look at

---

*Toril Moi reminds us that "in French there is only one adjective to 'femme' and that is 'feminin' whereas English has two adjectives to 'woman': 'female' and 'feminine'." (Moi p. 97). *Femininity*, as it is used in the translation of Cixous's text, is used in the sense of female, with no implications of the extraneous traces that femininity carries with it in English.

females in fiction from the perspective of recent critical theory, which means interrogating texts, and in relation to contemporary life. This spirit of vulnerable questioning rather than definitive answering is due in no small measure to the influence of feminism:

> Although feminist criticism might seem to threaten what is received by some critics as *truth*, it actually cannot threaten the academic critical establishment nor the history of criticism nor critical *truth*, if criticism is perceived as a process of constructing meaning rather than as a body of knowledge. This would mean that the measure of good criticism is the correctness and completeness of that process and not just the correctness of a fixed body of critical *facts*.[4]

It is my hope that this exploration of females in fiction will help us better understand the stories we have inherited, to seek new meanings and interpretations in them and to begin to tell new stories to ourselves and one another.

THE QUESTION OF QUESTIONING

When we examine literary meaning, we can do so from a wide spectrum of critical perspectives and arrive at an even greater variety of response. As Jacques Derrida shows, "No meaning can be determined out of context, but no context permits saturation."[5] (Derrida says that this is his starting point: "What I am referring to here is not richness of substance, semantic fertility, but rather structure, the structure of the remnant."[6]) We know that writers' intentionality, text , and readers' response are only the tip of the iceberg of meaning. There are three essential activities that impose order upon our sea of confusion. The first is reading. "The supposed skill of reading is actually based upon a knowledge of the codes that were operative in the composition of a text and the historical situation in which it was composed."[7] We need to understand the basic elements of narrative coding. This is one reason we need to read to very young children. Almost unconsciously the adult will explain the needed code to the child: "The ideal reader shares the author's codes and is able to process the text without confusion or delay. Such a reader constructs a whole world from a few indications, fills in gaps, makes temporal correlations, performs those essential activities that Umberto Eco has called writing *ghost chapters* and taking *infernal walks* all without hesitation or difficulties."[8]

The second activity is interpretation — text upon text.

> It is the feeling of incompleteness on the reader's part that activates the interpretive process.... We may *read* a parable for story but we must *interpret* it for the meaning.... We feel that interpretation is a higher skill than reading, and we value texts that require interpretive activity. This is, in fact, one way of defining literature, and it is one reason for preferring fictional texts to thematic texts, stories to essays.[9]

The third activity is *criticism*, the one with which we are primarily concerned.

> Criticism involves a critique of the themes developed in a given fictional text, or a critique of the codes themselves, out of which a given text has been constructed.... The most striking recent examples of this sort of critical work have come from feminists, but any group that has identified its interests as a class can mount a critical attack on a story's codes and themes from the position of its own system of values. This is so because fiction deals with types, with representative characters, and can thus be criticized only from a position correspondingly broad.[10]

Criticism must be made on behalf of a group, and many women now see themselves in this way. Scholes encourages us to "open the way between the literary or verbal text and the social text in which we live."[11] That is my critical and practical aim. As Virginia Woolf explains, "Masterpieces are not single or solitary births ... they are the outcome of thinking in common, of thinking by the body of the people, so that the experience of the mass is behind the single voice."[12] Thus, when we examine Austen's Emma, Hardy's Tess, James's Isabel, Laurence's Morag and Munro's Rose, we are hearing the voice of the mass. Each represents the situation, plight, struggle or triumph of many women. That Tess can only come alive by murder makes us tremble; she opens disturbing questions about the lives of women in all times and places. Emma's drawing-room confinement and concealment are not isolated phenomena brought about because she is motherless, comfortable and has a doting father. While Tess's spirit is broken only to rise with the thought of murdering the situation, Emma's must be curbed so that she may gain peace in the form of a suitable husband, her only safeguard from oblivion. Small wonder Rachel Blau DuPlessis noted the importance of *writing beyond the ending*. So often the end of the novel marked the very end of our lives. Emma Bovary's body dressed in her wedding gown at her funeral is an apt image: for women, marriage and death, the popular conclusions of our stories, have had many affinities.

When Isabel is trapped in a marriage to a sophisticated fortune-hunter who cares above all that appearances be preserved, she is representative. Female readers may long for the death of Gilbert Osmond so that the situation will be killed; their longing has implications beyond narrow textuality. When Morag marries one man, becomes pregnant by another and lives with neither of them, she is not alone, but representative of a ground swell of women who, while caring for commitment, challenge the conventional family unit. Rose's decision that finding out *who she thinks she is*, an important goal, signals a profound change in the way women are viewing and valuing themselves. Booky of *That Scatterbrain Booky*, Tony of *A Treasure for Tony* and Minerva of *The Minerva Program* all move in social texts filled with questions and implications. The meaning of these texts resides nowhere and everywhere, but certainly within the social structures that have produced and determined these female heroes. The questions each text asks may be as important as the questions we ask about it.

When we criticize we question the text, grappling with it until we ourselves produce meaning. This collaboration between reader and text may involve a solitary reader or a group of readers, but there is work to be done — meaning is being produced or, perhaps more accurately, being born. On her deathbed, Gertrude Stein is said to have drawn Alice Toklas to her to ask: "Alice, what is the answer?" Alice replies, "I'm afraid, Gertrude, we just don't know." After a pause, Gertrude brightens and asks, "Well then, Alice, what is the question?" Interrogating the text is an essential aspect of constructing its meaning.

Speaking of the use of fantasy by contemporary female writers, Patricia Stubbs says,

> Such a break is necessary if women are to be freed in literature from the closed world of private experience. . . . Only when novelists...are able to create women whose experience extends beyond the narrow limits of their own consciousness, beyond the personal world of human relationships and feelings, will this transformation come about. Thus it may be that what we require is more fiction and less realism.[33]

In Ursula LeGuin's *The Left Hand of Darkness*, everyone on the planet Gethen is both male and female, not in an androgynous sense, but alternately. No physiological habit is established, and the mother of several children may father several more. LeGuin insists that the Gethenians are a heuristic device, an experiment in thinking, a question. LeGuin's book tries to open up an alternative viewpoint, to widen the imagination.

> If men and women were completely and genuinely equal in their social roles, equal legally and economically, equal in freedom, in responsibility, and in self-esteem, then society would be a very different thing. What our problems might be, God knows. But it seems likely that our central problem would not be the one it is now: the problem of exploitation. Our curse is alienation. Divisions are insisted upon, interdependence is denied. The dualism of value that destroys us might give way to a much healthier, sounder, more promising modality of integration and integrity.[34]

Cheri Register has identified five functions literature must perform in order to be identifiably feminist. It must serve as a forum for women, help to achieve cultural androgyny, promote role models, promote sisterhood and augment consciousness-raising. Our analysis of the reading process shows, however, that a work standing alone does not necessarily perform any, let alone all, of these functions. Moreover, it may perform countless others that the feminist critic, when this term is applied in a reductionist manner, has not anticipated. Deconstruction has taught us not to depend exclusively on text, intention or response. Interpretation —selection, deletion, augmentation, reduction, exaggeration — will always come into play. Through reading, interpretation and criticism, any of our selected texts fulfills Register's demands. The provision of role models, too narrowly defined, would eliminate most literary works from consideration; however, when we employ the concept of différence, many, if not all, things immediately become possible.

Novels were first viewed as a great danger — almost as great a danger as information about contraception. Presenting females who took responsibility for their own lives and offering women control over their own bodies threatened the double standard. Before we celebrate our present enlightenment, we might remember that novels by Margaret Laurence are still being banned, and the opposition to family-planning courses continues.

There have been many cryptic comments about the shape and content of the novel being reducible to yells, bells and knells. Ezra Pound described it more elegantly as birth, copulation and death, but retained the Aristotelian shape of beginning, middle and end. The beginning, or birth, of the protagonist was rarely seen from the perspective of the woman giving birth. In fact, she regularly died during her "confinement": only the fruits of her labour were of real interest. (Fear of the female's creative powers has traditionally resulted in women being *confined* during some of their finest hours.) In *Portrait of a Lady*, neither Isabel's birth nor the birth of her child is given any attention. Isabel is one in the long line of protagonists, female and male, who have been conveniently orphaned. Giving birth and parenting have been given short shrift in the classic tradition. Giving birth, however, and what it means to the women who give it is now being addressed and explored in the novel; and the novel, while travailing and groaning, seems to be standing up under the strain. *The Honeyman Festival* is about carrying a child, delivering it — for it is the one who carries who also delivers — and being a mother.

Minn was in the bath, and filled the bath. The globe of her belly rose above the waterline to meet the spotted ceiling. She thought, it's going to be soon, or a very big kid. It won't hold on another six weeks. I won't stretch any farther, it's as far out as it was when the twins were in there. . . . As the water rose around her, the child kicked and plunged. She tapped it gently with an extended finger, to let it know how things would be if she had the strength. From conception, there was a relationship of sorts. She covered her belly with a wrung-out washcloth to keep it warm.[35]

▲

The story is still beginning on the final page:

Whatever happens, the universe will roll on somehow. It's big enough to do without us, there's a comfort. The tides will ebb and flow, the moon rise even if she isn't cheese or snow....And the morning will come, and so will the night again. Won't it?[36]

While women have been praised for a tidy house, their lives have often been anything but tidy, not only because of natural causes, such as menstruation, childbirth and lactation, but because creating a tidy life takes a ruthlessness they have lacked, an ability to say *no* to those in need. The senses of duty and caring extended to young and old have been well-developed among them; the more people you let into your life, the messier it becomes. The content of the novel — in exceptional cases in the eighteenth and nineteenth centuries and increasingly in the twentieth century — has become messy, as it holds the mirror up to women's lives.

Jane Austen implies that history may very well be a uniform drama of male posturing that is no less a fiction (and a potentially pernicious one) than Gothic romance. She suggests too that this fiction of history is finally a matter of indifference to women, who never participate in it and who are almost completely absent from its pages...like [Virginia] Woolf, Austen asserts that women see male-dominated history from the disillusioned and disaffected perspective of the outsider.[37]

The novel's contents are now spilling over, and writers such as Alice Munro, Mavis Gallant and Jean Rhys are challenging and breaking Aristotelian unities by the discontinuity of feminist thought and fiction. The stories of female heroes once ended with marriage — often the marriage hearse — or death, the glass coffin of masochistic revenge, the sickly beauty celebrated from Edgar Allen Poe to Louisa May Alcott. The stories of male heroes, on the other hand, have traditionally ended with success: the successful slaying of the dragon and the bedding of the beautiful maiden or the masterful rise to power and riches from poor and humble beginnings through true grit and industry.

We look at many women who endure, at those who do not marry and at those who find that there is indeed life after marriage. Perhaps most important, some of them discover that whatever befalls, they are interesting, independent individuals, not simply dim reflections of someone else.

The women we discuss get old, but they do not always conveniently die for narrative neatness and suitable symmetry. Like Aunt Dew of *The Hundred Penny Box*, they may reach five score years and keep on singing their songs. Some of these women are downtrodden but many shout with the unnamed hero of *Surfacing*, "This above all, to refuse to be a victim."[38] (While Emma has no story of her own, the hero of *Who Do You Think You Are?* is not compelled to depend on the stories of others: she constructs her own story.)

Women learn to differentiate between self-inflicted or ritual duties and genuine action. To the aesthete's narrow and petulant plea that content does not matter — that only the beauty of language and form concerns true literati — one can reply only that beautiful edifices are constructed of bricks and mortar, as beautiful people consist of blood and guts. Novels are powerful purveyors of ideas; beauty alone is not enough. In the end, art holds the mirror up to all aspects of life and all manner of women and men. In other words, the content absorbs us.

> Who cares about the text? We all do. We care about texts for many reasons, not the least of which is that they bring us news that alters our ways of interpreting things. If this were not the case, the Gospels and the teachings of Karl Marx would have fallen on deaf ears.[39]

They did not, because they were imaginative visions. We can look to the imaginative possibilities of the work of Margaret Laurence and Alice Munro, of Julia Kristeva and Gayatri Spivak. They will not fall on deaf ears because "textual power is ultimately power to change the world."[40] In the lives of females in fiction, art and life are indivisible. As Northrop Frye observes, "literature is itself an active part of the historical process."[41] Literature dictates, but it also reveals and offers possibilities. Stories provide ways of examining not only the mirroring of life in art, but also the normative impact of art on life.

The challenge to Robert Graves is long overdue. While *The White Goddess*, skilfully queried in fiction by Alice Munro, is scholarly in the patrician sense, it is primarily exasperating to the female reader. Is woman no more than this? Her reflection in the three-way man-made mirror renders three pictures and three pictures only, pictures in which we are seen most often as destructive and almost always to be feared: mother, temptress and hag are all defined by our relationships to men. Small wonder that slogans such as "Women Beware Women" could for so long divide us. Our prescribed masques of giving life and succour followed by sucking the vitality from our victims and visiting death upon them were sufficient to make us ashamed of ourselves and terrified of one other.

More central to our present preoccupation, however, is the notion that there is one story and one story only worth our telling: the male-hero story was long our standard text. It is difficult to shake off that conditioning, which spared us both decision and action. Heroes' stories are remarkably similar the world over. We, if we were conventionally beautiful and devoid of spirit, might look forward to sharing the spoils of the hero's quest, while we were ourselves despoiled. The rest of us played no part in the story at all.

Masques of Morality celebrates other masques. For, just as there is a different voice, so there is another story. It is to this other story, which is supremely worth our telling, that we will now turn.

THE QUESTION OF LANGUAGE

> The English language has been literally man made. . . . It is still
> primarily under male control. . . . This monopoly over language is
> one of the means by which males have ensured their own primacy,
> and consequently have ensured the invisibility or *other* nature of
> females, and this primacy is perpetuated while women continue to
> use, unchanged, the language which we have inherited.[13]

It is unlikely that most of us remember when we first realized
which sex we were: it seems as if we have always known; from
birth we are numbed by our naming as female or male. At birth,
socialization-according-to-gender engulfs us. Part of this socialization comes from stories: folk and family lore for virtually
everyone and the written and read tale or text for many of us.
School, of course, catches everyone up in print, and much of that
print presents stories. We get the way we are by imaging and
imagining: stories are the food and fuel for this process.
Didacticism, moralizing and the inculcation of ideology have
always been more pleasant when absorbed in the guise of a
rousing good yarn in which adult and child join in the delicious
conspiracy. When we examine the dynamic involved, however,
and deconstruct the language and thought of the content, a very
complex and influential power is exposed. Language differen-
tiates by an act of violence. Human beings may become human
through the acquisition of language, but both women and men
are almost inevitably diminished by the blinkers language
imposes.

Every society has a number of standard stories into which its
members are somehow supposed to fit. These stories enable and
discourage thought and action. They reward us for conforming
and punish us when we dream and live out stories that deviate too
far from the standard. All the fictional females we consider are
affected by the standard stories of their times. Some push old
stories to the limit; others insist that new stories be told and lived.
What we know is "not the world but stories about the world, . . .
no use of language matches reality but . . . all uses of language are
interpretations of reality."[14] While we all live in "the prison

house of language,"* it is certain that ". . . linguistically speaking, women are doubly disadvantaged in being, as it were, prisoners of the male prisoners in the prison house of language."[15]

Since our language not only defines but imprisons us, it is difficult to employ it to free ourselves from its chains. Only "by a continual process of defamiliarization can we ever hope to change. We begin by the exposing of conventions, the discovering of codes that have become so ingrained we do not notice them but believe ourselves to behold through their transparency the real itself."[16] The conventions involve deep structures, to be sure, yet it is surprising how much may be gained by analysing and reflecting upon surface talk and writ. The pen may indeed be mightier than the sword, but until recent times it has been almost exclusively men who have wielded both these phallic symbols. For example, talking "man to man" implies straightforward, honest discourse. "Woman to woman" suggests quite different meanings. Women's conversation is of no real value. "Talking constantly, women emitted chatter, gossip and foolishness. Gushing forth torrents of empty words, babbling contradictorily, all sense cancelled out, leaving merely noise."[17] Another deeply ingrained convention of woman's language is of woman the liar. According to this tradition, "Woman spoke, neither to enlighten with philosophy or science, nor to give her word as the guarantee for some joint enterprise; she spoke to deceive."[18] (One of the positive things that can be said for *Little Women* is that the members of the March family do talk to one another, and conversation is neither banal nor devalued because no male is on the scene.)

Pronouns are often the first element of conventional surface language that we notice. The charge that they are sexist is rarely harshly enough laid or seriously enough taken. "She" represents women. It can also, when pushed, represent ships and other machines that men control, or hurricanes and other disasters that men fear. "He," however, has the potency to represent the human race, the universal. "Generic *she* goes unnoticed: the same

---

*The reference is to *The Prison House of Language* by Fredric Jameson.

person who tells a class that '*he* must always be used when males are potential referents' can send a notice home informing parents of a 'teacher's expectations of her pupils' in a school where teachers of both sexes are employed."[19]

The possessive pronoun is deeply implicated as well. In Woolf's *The Years*, the patriarchal family is violently assaulted as the source of fascism. Marriage is a primitive form of private property." We will never be civilized as long as we wallow in the primeval swamp of marriage; if it is a question of my children, *my* property . . ."[20] Julia Kristeva points out that since God is love (and, we have been taught, male, as well), women are able to imagine *him* as a child. A child, after all, is a bundle of god-like unknown potential. Grown men are rarely god-like in the sense of incarnate love. "Here again," observes Kristeva, "one acknowledges the brilliant inspiration of the Christian religion."[21] Creators are male. Women are created from men with one part muted, mutilated or missing. Women are created by male language. Many studies have indicated that when "he" is used in a universal sense, males picture males, while females picture both males and females but with a preponderance of males in their imaging. The resistance of women to such obvious findings shows not only the power of unexamined convention but also the oft-documented resistance of slaves to notice, let alone throw off, their chains.

Binary opposition abounds, and the scales are usually tipped in favour of the male:

Man	Woman
Plus	Minus
Presence	Absence
Full	Empty
Good	Bad
Upright	Fallen
Strong	Weak

and so on.

To this we could add examples of what Cixous has called

patriarchal binary thought. Under the heading, "Where is he?" Cixous lines up the following oppositions.

Activity	Passivity
Sun	Moon
Culture	Nature
Day	Night
Father	Mother
Head	Emotions
Intelligible	Sensitive
Logos	Pathos[22]

The position of privilege in a list or sentence is in need of defamiliarizing. "Women, children and men," "sister and brother," may not "sound right," as we say. Was there anything right about the privilege "men" and "brother" enjoyed, shaping our thoughts as to which comes first? It is essential to depose the monarchs of semiotic privilege; binary oppositions may need to be outgrown. The following commonly used surface terms carry different innuendos when applied to females than when applied to males: aggressive, independent, stubborn, determined, broad-shouldered. "Swashbuckling," for example, is rarely applied to females, but "shrewish," "waspish," "fallen" and "strident" confirm the male-concocted notion that the female of the species is more deadly than the male.

Many nouns have a female form: heroine, actress, executrix. It is encouraging to note how rapidly these female forms are being expunged from the language. *Actress* is increasingly unpopular. Surely economic acumen and flawless integrity, not gender, are the significant attributes in a person to whom one entrusts one's affairs. The female, as in *ewe,* may persist, although it is unlikely that such labels will do irreparable damage to a little lamb's self-esteem, for animals, unless humans interfere, live in a state of nature: people do not. What is *natural* is beside the point: we live in a culture.

The terms *hero* and *heroine* have haunted the preparation and writing of this book. Clearly, the heroine's days are numbered. She may have to be a female hero while in transition, but it is likely that she will settle soon for being a hero, pure and simple. "Female writer" and "male writer" (the corresponding new term forced by feminist criticism), and an interesting abberation, women adopting male pseudonyms in order to be taken seriously, may eventually give way to the comprehensive term *writer*. We are in a self-conscious state about nomenclature. It is well worth the clumsiness and awkwardness we speak and feel and write, because we are on the move from unconscious conditioning and unquestioning acceptance to full consciousness. Waking can be painful but being wide awake is no mean goal. As long as society continues to divide itself along gender lines, language will support and challenge the status quo. I use "heroine," "female hero" and "hero" with lapses into "protagonist" and "character" in an effort to de-sex the jargon.

We need to be alert, analysing language in every sphere of life, lest we drowse back to semiotic abuse or self-abuse. The codification of female and male is sharply focused by Carol Gilligan in her penetrating plea that we listen to those — more than half the world — who yearn to speak in a different voice. Quoting from Erikson, Gilligan does not underestimate the difficulties:

> The Female holds her identity in abeyance as she prepares to attract the man by whose name she will be known, by whose status she will be defined, the man who will rescue her from emptiness and loneliness by filling *the inner space*. While for men, identity precedes intimacy and generativity in the optimal cycle of human separation and attachment, for women these tasks seem instead to be fused. Intimacy goes along with identity, as the female comes to know herself as she is known, through her relationships with others.[23]

Gilligan concludes, however, with an affirmation of the female life cycle, which displaces woman's place in man's cycle and declares her hope in the different voice of women:

> Yet in the different voice of women lies the truth of an ethic of care, the tie between relationship and responsibility, and the origins of aggression in the failure to connect. The failure to see the different realities of women's lives and to hear the differences

in their voices stems in part from the assumption that there is a single mode of human social experience and interpretation. By positing instead two different modes, we arrive at a more complex rendition of human experience, which sees the truth of separation and attachment in the lives of women and men and recognizes how these truths are carried by different modes of language and thought.[24]

It is precisely to the woman's cycle that we turn, with an awareness of the danger, both in fiction and in the world, that she can too easily fall back into her place in the male scheme of things.

Language is never value-free, and the question of language is one that we need to ask of every text. An important part of deconstructing narratives involves tearing apart linguistic masses. Stanley Fish suggests that changes in conventions of verbal expression are manifestations of the changes in belief that occur as a different social group assumes authority through struggle or persuasion. One standard story is replaced by another, and a different "truth" is created. The community is prior to the individual, truth or knowledge is human-made, and transformation is inevitable.

"i found god in myself . . . & i loved her fiercely"[25] sing the seven female actors in Ntozake Shange's *For Colored Girls Who Have Considered Suicide/When The Rainbow in Enuf*. Certainly god is female and male, but perhaps more important, when we consider the question of language, is our recognition of language's God-like power.

THE QUESTION OF CONTENT

Miriam, in Dorothy Richardson's *The Tunnel*, is shocked that an encyclopedia would have an entry headed "Woman," but she has also found the classics, the works in every field of knowledge, saturated with the opinion that women stopped being people. They were limited to their gynecological functions and stigmatized as "half-human, inferior, undeveloped" men. Because "Education would always mean coming in contact with all that,"

Miriam cries: "If one could only burn all the volumes of the encyclopedia, stop the publication of them. But it was all the books, all the literature in the world, right back to Juvenal."[26] All books seem to Miriam to perpetuate the notion of woman's inferiority. As long as the mirror continued to reflect a male view of the universe, a writer who did not want her own life script prepared by uncontrollable forces was bound to fantasize about book burning. It was not books themselves but their unrelenting ideology she longed to destroy.

Just as the power over words used and the use of those words is thought control, and as the voice, the point of view, is the privileged manipulation of content, so the content itself — the very shape and innards of written narrative — may be the construct of an exclusive view of the world. The description of Catherine Morland in *Northanger Abbey* might, with a few differences, describe Jo March or, more profitably still, that Scatterbrain Booky. Catherine was "fond of all boy's play, and greatly preferred cricket not merely to dolls, but to the more heroic enjoyments of infancy, nursing a dormouse, feeding a canary-bird, or watering a rose-bush. [She was] noisy and wild, hated confinement and cleanliness, and loved nothing so well in the world as rolling down the green slope at the back of the house."[27] Alas, indulgence is given to this passion for life only until a girl reaches her mid teens. Then, as did Catherine, she is likely, as Austen says, to "go into training for a heroine." Catherine began to curl her hair; dressing hair, as Alison Lurie points out in *The Language of Clothes*, may signal the end of female freedom. Lovers and husbands prefer long hair, which is sexy and sensuous; male employers prefer short hair, which is neat and efficient. Unless we carefully deconstruct the situation, the only choice is which males the female should placate. "The killing of oneself into an art object — the pruning and preening, the mirror madness, and concern with odours and aging, with hair which is inevitably too curly or too lank, with bodies too thin or too thick —all this testifies to the efforts women have expended not just trying to be angels but trying not be monsters."[28]

Increasingly, however, women are refusing to pretend, as

Isabel Archer does," that there is less of her than there is." Morag, in spite of her husband's demands, refuses to go to that narcissistic masochistic house of mirrors ironically labelled the beauty parlour. In an effort to efface or conceal what society considers the ravages of time, time is endlessly squandered. While many women succumb to present-day formula romances, many others are refusing to diminish themselves by aping the stock characters of these addictive stories. In cataloguing the attributes of the heroine of present-day romance, Kathryn Weibel notes:

> ... the hero is usually about ten years older than the heroine ... and of higher social or economic status . . . the hero is much more aggressive and self-confident than the heroine . . . he appears to hold the upper hand in any disagreement with the heroine, and he is frequently curt or sharp in his speech with the heroine.... In short, the hero wins out over rivals by superiority; the heroine, it would seem, by inferiority.[29]

These formulae *prescribe* appropriate behaviour for female readers at least as much as they *describe* it. Not only do these depictions of young women signal the death of spontaneity and the stunting of growth; they condemn to feelings of inferiority and inadequacy the women who buy into the system. Failure to measure up to the set piece is almost guaranteed.

These images of women in fiction bear some relation to many of the characters we will discuss. Tatterhood of folk tale refuses to wear the fancy garb or to allow an interest in appearance to consume her. The Mum in *The Gifts of War* dresses up and beds down with a prince of her own concocting: she wakes up with a toad. If stories about women end either with marriage or death, the questions, "What will she do now, poor thing?" or "What would have happened had she lived?" are bound to be asked. And, of course, contemporary literature is now responding to them. "After the kids are all in school, the dreary mums bloom again. They get new clothes and sprint from job to job singing. It works until they collide with paranoid teenagers and fall back, mortally wounded."[30] The artist is the only woman who seems to be able to get off the wheel that hurtles women to the feared and dreaded position of hag. Yet they are disparaged as second rate, because sexually they are second class. "No happy woman writes!" "In creation, in synthesis, in criticism, in pure intellect women, even the most exceptional and the most favoured, have never approached the accomplishment of men."[31] Lilly, the artist in *To the Lighthouse*, raises profound questions, as do the many female writers among fictional heroes. Emily of *I Stand Here Ironing,* and Rose, partly escape the cruel continuum through their art as actors. Morag of *The Diviners* becomes part of a more promising genre in which the heroine goes on a quest that is primarily spiritual.

> A number of older women, having lived through various feminine and masculine roles and having rejected a good many social expectations, attain a state of unity with the green world and with the universe. These heroes have experienced a transformation of the personality, a centering upon personal rather than patriarchal space that differentiates them from the younger heroes of the novel of development.[32]

▲

CHAPTER TWO

WHAT IS
TO BE DONE?

The glory of man is knowledge, but the glory of woman is to renounce knowledge.

THIS AXIOM, BELIEVED TO HAVE ORIGINATED in ancient China, is still subscribed to in blatant or subtle forms in most countries and cultures. Throughout history and literature woman has been portrayed as a time-wasting creature whose value is chiefly ornamental, or as one whose work consists of menial or non-essential tasks. When women enter any field in significant numbers, the status of that group is likely to plummet. Women have been stereotyped as overwrought or flighty, and they are usually described by their condition (daughter, spinster, wife, mother) rather than their work. They have been effectively cut off from power and decision making. Traps may be vicious or tender, cages steel or golden, but the confinement is inescapable. The vices in which women find themselves will be based on gender but are likely to be compounded by socio-economic level, colour, age, religion and the determinism of time and place. There is no evidence that women crave accomplishment and the self-esteem that accompanies it any less than men, in spite of society's penchant for directing females to bask only in the reflected glory of fathers, husbands and progeny. Given the traditional chasm between societal expectations and our longing to get the work done, it is small wonder that many women have emphasized not rumination and speculation but determining "What is to be done?"

In this chapter, all the females find themselves in a state of tension. They have lively imaginations and are not content with the status quo. They all know that something must be done and, for better or worse, they act upon that knowledge.

Emma, written in 1816, asks serious questions about the way society is ordered to the built-in disadvantage of women. Emma has few outlets for her talents and vivacity, so she tampers with other people's lives. She is plagued by the lack of substance and choice in her life. While her circumstances in no way justify her meddling, Emma's predicament raises profound social questions. Is it ethical to deliberately waste female potential in the service of a stable, patriarchal order? Admittedly, Emma's actions very nearly cause tragedy for herself and her friends. While her circumscribed daily existence cannot excuse her playing puppeteer to her neighbours, it goes a long way towards explaining her behaviour. The fact that Emma concocts stories about the lives of others focuses our attention on the sad fact that she has no real story of her own. This need for a story of one's own raises serious questions about the position of females in all times and places.

Moll Flanders, whose beginnings are precarious, to say the least, must decide what is to be done again and again. She must act decisively to ensure mere physical survival in the political and economic jungle of her society. Sometimes, because of insufficient data or unfortunate timing, she does not decide wisely, but these occasions demonstrate, for Defoe, writing in 1722, and for the reader of today, the extent to which she and women like her are pawns of patriarchy's rich and powerful. Moll cannot continue to conform to the social system or it will crush her. She uses her wits to move outside it, to exercise some degree of self-determination, first for survival and then so that she may flourish and prosper. The temptations and trappings of her setting have unsuspected and unsettling parallels with our own.

The Country Bunny asks what is to be done if you are brown, rural and female in a world controlled by white urban males. Within such severe limitations, she determines what she can do. The impressive combination of hope, self-esteem, imagination and industry by which the country bunny implements what is to be done places her among the many female animal characters in fiction who provide fascinating cultural insights and compelling role models.

The Well-Worn Path demands a close textual reading, thanks to Eudora Welty's writing skill. Phoenix, an old black woman, decides what is to be done because, strong and courageous as she is, she can do nothing else. Circumstances, need and unconditional caring ensure that she, like so many women, will do what she must.

In *That Scatterbrain Booky*, Booky and her family have a difficult time unscrambling what is to be done in the midst of the Depression. Fixed sex roles made deciding what to do both relatively simple and impossibly difficult. Escaping some sex-role prescription by refusing marriage indicates that there is more latitude for the middle class than Emma could have foreseen. What is to be done in the face of unemployment, inadequate birth control, debt and family tension is a question that many people today must answer under conditions not always very different from those of Booky's household.

In these novels, and those listed in the appendix, females find themselves constrained by societal shackles at almost every turn. Nevertheless, the imagination and gumption they display provide inspiration and hope that women will yet discover what is to be done to bring us into the full humanity we all deserve.

EMMA
by
JANE AUSTEN

After *Pride and Prejudice*, *Emma* is Austen's most discussed and analysed novel. Its heroine, whom Jane Austen feared "no one but herself would like," is the central presence in a novel that is essential to the study of the masques of morality in the English novel, social history and feminist thought. *Emma* has recently been enjoyed by an increasingly wide and varied readership.

> Since a novel has this correspondence to real life, its values are to some extent those of real life. But it is obvious that the values of

women differ very often from the values which have been made by the other sex. The whole structure, therefore, of the nineteenth-century novel was raised, if one was a woman, by a mind which was slightly pulled from the straight, and made to alter its clear vision in deference to external authority . . . . What genius, what integrity it must have required in the face of all that criticism, in the midst of that purely patriarchal society, to hold fast to the thing as they saw it without shrinking. Only Jane Austen did it and Emily Bronte. It is another feather, perhaps the finest, in their caps.[1]

Whether there is at all times and in all places a distinctly female voice or vision in art has still to be determined. However, as Virginia Woolf exclaimed, Jane Austen "got it right" and "kept it straight." Austen was not a fool of her time. She simply depicted it in clearer detail and sharper focus than almost anyone else. She held fast to the thing as she saw it, ignoring the admonitions of any "external pedagogue." "Jane Austen turned her creative energies to the reformation of propriety in the hope of finding within its codes an acceptable form for a woman's desires and a reinforcement for the social order she cherished."[2]

Much has been made, by recent critics, of Jane Austen's literary erudition. Unlike Emma, who, according to Mr. Knightly, made all the right lists, Austen read the right books. It is amazing, given the inevitable interruptions, the domestic responsibilities, and her untimely death that Austen read to such enormous effect and wrote with such compression and craft. (While *Emma* should never be mistaken for a rewriting of *A Midsummer Night's Dream*, there are nonetheless enough striking parallels — near-fatal mistakes, "lifted language," weather conditions with implicit symbolism culminating in satisfying and shapely endings — to have warranted significant scholarship about the effects of one upon the other wrought in the crucible of the Austen imagin-ation. The measured movements of a dance in the forest enclo-sure is not as obviously confining as a drawing room, nor as claustrophobic; yet the dream itself is hermetic.) The point is simply that her place both as a writer of exquisite cameos and as a part of the mainstream of literary development is assured. Her work issues from a rich English tradition; later writers learned from her thought and are still writing in her debt.

Austen revealed the economic basis of all human intercourse. As Hardy was later to lament, "Everything looked like money." In the twentieth century, Auden observed:

> You could not shock her more than she shocks me;
> Beside her Joyce seems innocent as grass.
> It makes me most uncomfortable to see
> An English spinster of the middle class
> Describe the amorous effects of 'brass',
> Reveal so frankly and with such sobriety
> The economic basis of society.[3]

Even Knightly's support of Martin, the striving gentleman farmer, is conditional upon Martin's "promise" to Knightly that he could "afford it."[4] However limited, this support is one of the strongest breakthroughs in the stifling class structure in *Emma*. Mr. Knightly, although supposedly a proponent of social reform, asks heatedly, "What are Harriet Smith's claims of birth or nature or education? . . . She is the natural daughter of nobody knows whom, with probably no settled provision at all and certainly no respectable relations."[5] Emma, possessive and wishing to outfox the system, seizes upon the only vehicle at hand, the marriage carriage, in order that her friend's lot may be improved materially and socially. That she seriously violates a moral system need not mask her obvious impatience with the attendant socio-economic one. Perhaps the most redeeming feature of the world Austen depicts is the open acknowledgement of the importance of money in domestic affairs. It may be that more human pain has been engendered by the tortuous and complicated credo of Gilbert Osmond, "Money is a vulgar thing to follow, but a charming thing to meet," than by the open admission that a certain pride and prejudice and a certain number of pounds per year are prerequisites for domestic felicity.

"Jane Austen has always been famous for fireside scenes in which several characters comfortably discuss options so seemingly trivial that it is astonishing when they are turned into important ethical dilemmas."[6] No matter how small the physical or social world of the novel or of life, these ethical dilemmas torment and tantalize. Deportment and social graces are consciously cultivated and Emma makes much of them in everyone who comes under her influence. *Emma*, as surely as any novel in the language, concentrates on polished manner masking sullied morality, and upon crude manners concealing worthy character. It is also about the combination of fine morals and manners of Mrs. Weston, the inferior manners and morals of Mr. Woodhouse, and about the occasions when, for the sake of morality, manner may be overridden as in the harsh, but accurate, estimate Knightly gives of his beloved's moral code.

Emma has been to the manner born and yet is constantly confusing manners with morality and misplacing moral emphases. For example, after the success with Miss Taylor and Mr. Weston, Emma turns her attention to Harriet Smith and Mr. Elton. That Mr. Martin loves Harriet and Harriet is not insensitive to his advances is merely an impediment to be overcome.

> The older a person grows, Harriet, the more important it is that their manners should not be bad; the more glaring and disgusting any loudness, or coarseness, or awkwardness becomes. What is passable in youth is detestable in later age. Mr. Martin is now awkward and abrupt; what will he be at Mr. Weston's time of life? . . . He will be a completely gross, vulgar farmer, totally inattentive to appearances and thinking of nothing but profit and loss . . . his being illiterate and coarse need not disturb us.[7]

The manners of Mr. Elton, whose morals are decidedly inferior to those of the maligned Mr. Martin, are, in Emma's estimation, a model of perfection: "I think a young man might be very safely recommended to take Mr. Elton as a model. Mr. Elton is good-humoured, cheerful, obliging and gentle."[8]

Emma, who at twenty-one has health, beauty, charm, intelligence, artistic talent, material wealth and the relative freedom of being mistress in her father's house, is not as compelled to marry as are her less fortunate "sisters." She has many material advantages over Elizabeth Bennet of *Pride and Prejudice* — the absence of an obsessive mother and four sisters of "marriageable age" not least among them — but they do share certain features. Emma and Elizabeth are less than anxious to marry, feeling themselves in understanding and outlook superior to other women; and both are loved by fathers with whom they have exceptionally close relationships. Both learn that they are capable of a stronger affection and achieve in their marriages something closer to what feminists today would call "mutuality" than was possible for most women of their time. Emma's marriage fits a modern arrangement more closely: Knightly agrees to move, after all, from his fine ancestral home to make life more agreeable for Mr. Woodhouse and, thus, for Emma. Emma, from her reading of romance and ruin, knows full well how remote the possibility of finding a suitable mate really is. She has no economic or social need to marry and knows how rare are the men who might interest her.

> There are such beings in the World, perhaps one in a thousand, as the creature you and I should think perfection, where Grace and Spirit are united to Worth, where the Manners are equal to the Heart and Understanding, but such a person may not come in your way, or if he does, he may not be the eldest son of a Man of Fortune, the Brother of your particular friend, and belonging to your own Country.[9]

Austen adds to all these objective characteristics the "power of attaching" one, subjective feelings of sexual attraction. The mating equation seems increasingly unlikely to balance.

For women less fortunate in circumstances and personal power, marriage remains the "only honorable provision for well-educated young women of small fortune, their pleasantest preservation from want."[10] The sexual and economic strictures of patriarchy force women to marry, teach school or be governesses, related, subservient activities in Austen's context; the women themselves, however, are of no interest after they marry.

Today's heroine, of course, can rekindle social attention through separation, divorce and renewed speculation about her mating habits. The contemporary novel would ask what kind of marriage Elizabeth and D'Arcy might really have. Would Emma, contrite and cleansed, continue to find her love for Mr. Knightly the emotion of which she is "most proud"? "There is no happiness in love, except at the end of an English novel," observed Trollope. However, marriage no longer strikes the same note of finality in the story of a woman's life. With luck one may continue to be defined by who one is, what one knows and what one does, rather than by to whom, or worse, to what, one is married. "The idea of finding oneself by finding one's husband is widely disbelieved. But the subtler fantasy the English novelists nourish is harder to shake: the inclination to see oneself as a heroine."[11]

Because Emma had no scope for a life of her own, we are ambivalent about the extent of her depravity in toying with the lives of others. Mr. Woodhouse holds her on a short leash, much as Adam Verver holds Charlotte Stant in *The Golden Bowl*. They must both sing for their suppers — an even and a pleasing song. Charlotte at least gets a sumptuous meal for her efforts, but Emma's meals are somewhat Spartan. Selfishly, Mr. Woodhouse protests that it is out of consideration for his guests that he does not encourage them to eat. For Emma, as for everyone, gruel has its limitations and wine tastes better from a generously filled glass. All the social events, the calls and the visits that provide some structure and meaning to Emma's life, are, with the exception of walks with a female companion, dependent upon the largesse and cooperation of males.

There are a number of reasonably considerate sons, brothers, suitors, husbands and fathers in the novel, but the extreme dependency of even the most independent female is demeaning: the sixteen miles to London might be six hundred without a man to take charge of horse and carriage to convey one there. Throughout the novel Emma must prevail upon her father, who dislikes all forms of travel, to visit their relatives and neighbours. The getting there, which might provide half the fun, is often full of stress engendered by Mr. Woodhouse's petty anxieties. In this regard, Emma and her female contemporaries of the gentry are less fortunate than the poorest man among them, who may walk to London if he wishes. (Are there traces of this unwelcome legacy in the lack of freedom women still feel to travel unescorted on our city streets?) For Austen, the extreme confinement of women is a condition of life.

It is a moot point, too, whether the strict observance of the elaborate system of manners and etiquette, which characters flout at their peril, really adds grace and kindness to social proceedings. There is no question that it facilitates misunderstanding and, when the characters desire it, deception. Most of the letters in the novel, for example, contain "nothing but truth, though there might be some truths not told." The fine line between tempering truth with mercy, a necessity for civilized social intercourse, and falsehood is blurred quite regularly in *Emma*. Emma discovers "the ambiguous nature of discourse that mystifies, withholds, coerces and lies, as much as it reveals."[12] "Seldom, very seldom," Austen reminds us, "does complete truth belong to any human disclosure; seldom can it happen that something is not a little disguised or a little mistaken."[13]

While, as one young reader remarked, everyone in an Austen novel is "on the make," it is sometimes difficult to decide who or what is the object of the commotion; certainly somebody is always in the dark. Austen knows, and by hints, guesses and signs often lets the alert reader into her confidence. It is this guessing game in which the reader must be constantly active, gauging the significance and weighing the meaning of every word and nuance, that yields much of what Roland Barthes has called "the pleasure of the text." Austen always stimulates the reader to supply what is not there. It is this engagement with the text, the sense of creating it at the point of reading and never quite pinning it down, that accounts in large measure for Austen's readers returning in droves to her polished gems throughout their lives.

As readers try to unearth just who the real Emma is, we discover that her manners are by no means always perfect; "she behaves rudely, making uncivil remarks at Box Hill, when she talks indiscreetly, unwittingly encouraging the advances of Mr. Elton" (whom she has planned, in her bounty, to bestow upon Harriet) and "when she allows her imagination to indulge in rather lewd suppositions about the possible sexual intrigues of Jane Fairfax and a married man."[14] Eventually Emma's manners do improve, and she becomes more ladylike and submissive; but do these "improvements," as Jane Austen may wish us to perceive them, signify a moral improvement as well? When Emma is brought up short with what her meddling has come to and how the trouble she has caused is averted in the nick of time, no thanks to her, her moral awareness and self-knowledge are augmented. Was it necessary, however, for her to become so much like Jane Fairfax, a morally superior Emma who has not been so indulged and spoiled? The contemporary reader may hate to accept that gaiety, spontaneity and outrageous wit must be sacrificed for moral improvement.

Must anyone "grow up" so completely? Does growing up mean surrendering exuberant imagination, or does it mean that such imagination has to be repressed into an acceptable and, above all, inoffensive code? Could Emma afford the luxury of saying what she meant? Can anyone? Perhaps the greatest hope for the union between Emma and Knightly lies in the truth, far greater than Emma intended, of her quip to her father that "We always say what we like to one another."

Emma, armed with charm and intelligence, marshals words and paint and pianoforte to add zest to her life. Her desire for diversion and power leads her to control the lives of others, for life is flat without a "project." In another time and place, we salute the woman who is not content to be, but insists on doing, on literally creating her own life. How harsh can we be in our condemnation of Emma? As she asks Mr. Knightly, is there not "a something between the do-nothing and do-all?" Emma may be the consummate playwright, manipulating others as characters; yet, except for placating Mr. Woodhouse, she has little else to do. Her repeated efforts to be both director and leading lady as well become more intelligible when one considers the blandness of the alternatives.

Emma's blindness to motives and feelings, including her own, holds the reader: its dissipation is, indeed, a moment of moral understanding and enlightenment. The haughty young woman who claimed she could not call on Harriet Martin has been outgrown. Whereas, in *Tess of the D'Urbervilles*, all things conspire to thwart Tess's best intentions and innocent actions, Mrs.

Weston's prophecy seems fulfilled: Emma will, indeed, make "no lasting blunder."

Nowhere is the interplay between outward form and morality more fascinating than in *Emma*. A modern-day Emma would doubtless appear talented but scheming and manipulative —the fundamentally unpleasant do-gooder we have learned to distrust. Her need to become involved in the lives of others far exceeds the admonition to be one's sister's keeper; such interference is all the more dangerous in the guise of selflessness and caring. Yet Emma's charms appeal to us as they do to Mr. Knightly; we delight in her even though we share his awareness of her shadier personal dealings. A charitable view would see her more as victim than villain in a society in which to be female is to be ancillary. As Emma has no personal quest, and because imagination will out, she spins tales about the lives in her tiny, suffocating milieu. She emerges as a woman of spirit, coming to terms with the art of the possible. Her reunion with her society and its standards and assumptions is the only happy ending possible, given the time and the setting.

> . . . by focusing on courtship, the myth of romantic love tends to freeze the relationship between a man and a woman at its moment of greatest intensity . . . when women seem to exercise their greatest power. Romantic love seems to promise to women an emotional intensity that ideally compensates for all the practical opportunities they are denied.[15]

When we drag Emma into the twentieth century, several things happen. We see how humiliating and debilitating Emma's circumstances must have been even for fortunate females such as she. We also see how much and how little things have changed. Economic conditions always affect the position and treatment of women. Married women of what was pointedly called "child-bearing age" were long denied work in many spheres, provided their husbands were, as the equally pointed phrase ran, "able-bodied." This situation obtained until the desperate days of World War II when men, able-bodied or otherwise, were in such short supply that even married women had to be pressed into service. The ideal of the "natural" or "normal" woman changed surprisingly little as a result of wartime exigencies. Attitudes about woman's place have altered, however, in the past two decades, but they are under attack again. Today, the law of supply and demand has been somewhat reversed and the rumblings against married women in the work force have resumed, in very nearly the rhetoric of yesteryear. The blind, weak, insensitive and chauvinistic men surrounding Emma have survived only thinly disguised and dislocated. So too do the descendants of the silly, superficial females in Austen novels who never rebel even in adolescence, and who never question the rightness of things as they are. (An education student described her professional studies as "something to do while the guy I live with finishes law school." How different is she from the Austen females who married to escape becoming governesses? How cheaply we still hold the nurturing and education of the young!)

Only by looking at other cultures, other times, other standards, other assumptions, can we measure, assess, understand or change our own. Self-consciousness liberates Emma from herself, enabling her to be sensitive and responsive to the needs of others. For Austen, selfishness and selflessness are virtually interchangeable: we cannot help but admire her portrayal of this principle at work within the bounds of the social contract. It is a delightful contrast to modern self-help books. Literature retains the beautifully turned phrase and the memorable incarnation of character so sadly lacking in the narcissism of self-help. Women have no monopoly on being thwarted, blocked, humiliated, repressed, disappointed, frustrated and defeated. One of the humiliations society inflicts upon its males is sending them to war. We use our sons as "cannon fodder" or, more recently, as "expendable grunts."(We ache with the father in Bernard Slade's play *Same Time Next Year* who says that since his son's death in Viet Nam, "it's just been one damn thing after another.") The pain that is based on gender however, whereby brothers may hope and sisters dare not, carries its own agony and tension, which Jane Austen can help us to understand. Some twentieth-century women are only too happy to resolve matters the way Emma eventually does: using passivity to steal power, submitting in order to control — all without questioning the secondary nature of being female. Others are not. A study of literature, of former times and other places as well as of recent times and North American locales, is perhaps the most fair and open avenue upon which we can meet ourselves and each other as we ponder "what is to be done."

MOLL FLANDERS
by
DANIEL DEFOE

When the novel first appeared in eighteenth-century England, it was met with cries that it was not literature at all, and allegations that it corrupted the morals of women. The modern way of seeing the universe, as Erica Jong points out, is in terms of the individual having some control of his or her destiny through his or her actions.[16] In this sense, Moll is modern: she does her best to take control of her life and shape her destiny against very tough odds. The rise of the middle class and of bourgeois consciousness is implicit in the quantification of everything in life. This novel is about Moll Flanders, but it is also about the society that produces her and assaults her and with which, after many a struggle, she comes to terms. "Heartless she is not nor can anyone charge her with levity; but life delights her . . . . Moreover, her ambition has that slight strain of imagination in it which puts it in the category of the noble emotions."[17]

Defoe was ahead of his time: he thought it appalling that women did not have men's opportunities for education. Defoe "creates a female character who is as adventurous and courageous as any man, but who is also honest and straight forward in a way we find very contemporary."[18] Moll, beginning as an outcast, eventually beats social, economic, political and, in a sense, theological forces. She tells her own story and we see the world through her eyes. She is neither graceful nor rebellious by nature, although she certainly rebels. She simply has to decide "what is to be done" in successive crises. That everything, including a human life, can be weighed and measured and its price assessed is the theme of the book. Is Moll victim or victor? Clearly she is both, but the question is open to a wide variety of interpretations. For the person who begins life on such a tenuous footing, security often becomes the ultimate life goal. Defoe knew well that it is easier to be virtuous with a bank account. The middle class, about whom he writes, hopes that with bank accounts the poor will remain virtuous and, as a result, not threaten the prevailing social structure. (Most welfare systems, however inadequate and iniquitous, are based upon this premise.) Defoe wishes that society were less savage. He shows us Moll dealing with the social jungle in the only ways that are possible and practical for her survival. Despite the fact that she flouts conventional morality, we sympathize with her and loathe the system that abuses her. When it seems that nothing can be done, Moll thinks of something; whatever means she must employ, she does so, regardless of the implications. Defoe shows us his time — and perhaps something of our own — through the life and times of the unsinkable Moll Flanders.

THE COUNTRY BUNNY AND THE LITTLE GOLD SHOES
by
DUBOSE HEYWARD

Mother Cottontail has three strikes against her. She is brown, she is from the country and, of course, she is female. Small wonder, then, that "all of the big white bunnies who lived in fine houses, and the Jack Rabbits with long legs who can run so fast, laughed at the little cottontail and told her to go back to the country and eat a carrot." Mother Cottontail is a single mother, coping on her own — with twenty-one offspring. An accepting and gracious parent, she instills self-reliance and artistic skills in her young.

She doesn't accept the fact that one must be male, white and urban to attain the highest position in the land, that of Easter Bunny. But, more than that, Mother Cottontail grapples with the question, "What is to be done?" How does one keep alive dreams of achievement and fulfilment when one has, literally or metaphorically, "twenty one cottontail babies to take care of"? Mother Cottontail is a supermom, but this book was written in 1939. From 1939 to 1945 — and to some extent ever since — women have had to be supermoms. Wartime conditions were long considered anomalous, but it is generally accepted that a return to circumscribed pre-war sex roles and unrelieved paternalism is impossible. Like many a shift worker, Mother Cottontail must work, and work around the times she is needed at home. She must also accept guidance and help from the "wise old grandfather bunny," family patriarch, company president or school inspector. She may become a priest, but it is futile to dream of being bishop: there *are* limits! DuBose Heyward and Marjorie Flack, however, assign to Mother Cottontail the place in the sun, and the other four Easter Bunnies become a composite token male. Yet, even though Mother Cottontail possesses remarkable vitality and imagination, it is only after her children are half grown, and in time sandwiched between her duties as mother, that she undertakes her quest and has her great adventure, attaining her goal. Considering its multiple meanings and the thousands of children to whom it is read, this "little animal story" cannot be regarded lightly.

THE WORN PATH
by
EUDORA WELTY

The Worn Path is a short story, rich in detail and sustained tension. Phoenix is a very old black woman who is wise and courageous and, most of all, determined. She can hardly make the trip to town for her grandson's medicine; but, at the end of the story, we feel certain, although Welty gives us no direct assurance, that in spite of difficult terrain, dogs that force her to lose her footing and streams that must be forded, Phoenix will make it back along that well-worn path to the waiting boy. Phoenix transcends correct behaviour. Her morality is so fundamental that her responses are automatic.

The white man she meets pulls her out of the ditch, compassionate to a point, but for the fun of it, he points his gun at her. The social worker in the welfare agency where Phoenix must go for her grandson's medicine has little patience with the old lady who cannot give her history. Even the nurse, who knows her, does not remain patient long. Old people, through fatigue and what the young would call overload, can be exasperating in their moments or hours of forgetfulness. Phoenix rises from her falls as the mythical bird from its ashes. She is indefatigable: however weak her body becomes, she does, by the strength of her spirit, something that she knows at a very deep level she must do. We recognize the white man's generalization about "colored people" to be vicious and racist; it becomes ironic, too, when we learn the purpose of Phoenix's trip down the well-worn path. The sources of the two nickels in the story make a telling comparison and Phoenix's quick decision about how to spend them might seem simply sentimental handled by a lesser writer than Welty.

The story line is simple, but the implications of *The Worn Path* are complex: the path is worn by Phoenix's repeated journeys; the treatment she receives because of the externals of age, sex and race is the path that many people must tread each day. In the particular travels of Phoenix, we read the painful story of a large portion of humanity. In her steadfast courage we see a measure of hope.

THAT SCATTERBRAIN BOOKY
by
B.T. HUNTER

Booky is set in the Dirty Thirties, a tale of long ago for children today. The realism of the text appears to be relieved by its setting in the past in that the expectations of the time are different. Yet the position of women and children, for example, is not as radically different as it may at first seem. When the family can no longer hide from the bailiff because of unpaid rent, Booky's mother "starts in on" her father.

> "I'm sick and tired of hiding from the bailiff and scaring the living daylights out of these children . . . And for two cents I'd go out and get a job myself.". . . That made Dad boil, because in those days a man would have to be a cripple in a wheel chair before he'd let his wife go out to work. So what followed was their biggest fight ever.[19]

Some things are changing: it is no longer acceptable to think of people in wheelchairs as cripples who can't work, and most men would hesitate before talking about *letting* their wives work outside the home. Yet many men in positions of power today are products of that time when no self-respecting man would let his wife work. Everyone, including the housebound wife, considered him responsible, a decent man and a good provider. A small percentage of families, only some of whom can afford the luxury, still think this way, and there are certain stresses they escape with this model. As many of the stories we examine indicate, a working mother must often do two jobs — one away from home, for which she is paid, and another at home, unpaid and unsung. Because she has some money of her own she may have a degree of power and influence in decision making, but often she feels chronic guilt and fatigue. Two full-time jobs are too much! "Work when you can get it from eight to six, six days a week," followed by work in the home without help, cannot be idealized even by distance. Because many of the attitudes of Booky's time persist today, it is important to locate their origins, examine them and work to change them. Otherwise many women will simply be too weary to clap hands and sing any song of liberation, and our dream of entering into full humanity will recede once again.

There is no question that matters are more complicated now. Many women feel that there is no more reason for them to choose between having children and having a job outside the home than there is for a man to make this choice. Society has no right to ask a woman why she works: the question is never addressed to a man. During the thirties, not long ago in terms of social history, the choice was inescapable. There are hints in the "biggest fight ever" of what we all know to be true, that, like Lottie, many women have always chosen the "single life" because they were not fearful of social censure and because they had "good heads on their shoulders."[20] It is certain that more imaginative ways of sharing responsibilities and satisfactions will have to be worked out between the sexes.

Booky helps us to understand that the experience of the thirties had profound and lasting effects. It turned some people into greedy misers and others into social activists. Both groups were motivated by the fear of "It" happening again. A society that could allow widespread hunger and produce sudden prosperity by waging war is one whose basic assumptions need questioning.

The triumphs of the human spirit and of familial love are the delight of the book and, of course, the child's view of growing up in the thirties is immediate and engaging. The details of advertising, the Santa Claus parade, the Dundas streetcar, Cabbagetown and Swansea lend a verisimilitude that takes us back even if we were never there before. The experience of childbirth at home in Toronto is one we must go to books to experience. As home births return, we can be sure they are being handled differently from those in this story.

Booky is an interesting character. Her ideas and behaviour quickly belie her nickname, Scatterbrain. She, like Lottie, has a good head on her shoulders. Imagination does not cast out intelligence — but it does lead her to a moral dilemma. She certainly inconveniences others and she is selfish, but she is also warm and loving and caring:

> Of course I wasn't allowed to go to bed dirty, far from it. I guess my mother was the cleanest woman in the world, but when she sent me up to take a bath, and after Dad had lugged a boilerful of scalding water up two flights of stairs, I'd just sit on the toilet seat day-dreaming and yanking on the chain of the water closet overhead listening to "Niagara Falls." Then, when the water in the tub had turned stone cold, I'd pull the plug, give my hands "a lick and a promise," put on my clean nightdress and hop happily into bed. Poor Willa. How she wished I had been born a boy so I would have to sleep with Arthur.[21]

Many true confessions may be elicited from the reader of this passage, regardless of the reader's age or sex. Boys' antipathy to water and cleanliness has been much celebrated; it is part of being a spirited boy. The honest admission that cleanliness is no more natural for girls than boys is refreshing.

Booky is irrepressible and her fears regularly give way to schemes and hope. Although the family unit moved from crisis to crisis, as it does now, *Booky* is a story of survival, the survival of the appetite for life. It declares that hope will triumph and that, all evidence to the contrary, set-backs will be temporary. We often know they will not, yet we believe they will. This, too, is a moral stance. The hope incarnate in Booky is a principle too often neglected: she shows us what is to be done.

▲

CHAPTER THREE

CAN ANYTHING BE DONE?

"CAN ANYTHING BE DONE?" is more than a question: it is a cry that echoes through the ages. In this chapter all masques are interrogated — society, politics, religion, systems of morality and, of course, the texts themselves. The clash between the sexes, in which woman must bear public censure and private guilt while man somehow largely escapes both, is exposed. The horrifying inevitability and the readiness with which society would make woman both victim and guilty is relentless and depressing. With a legacy such as this, can anything be done?

Tess of the D'Urbervilles captures, more than any other work we will discuss, the prevalent and nonsensical notion of the natural woman, a woman who is one with the open fields and with the cycle of the natural world. Neither Tess nor any woman is any such thing. We live in a particular culture, and society pushes, cajoles, forces, dislocates us into an acceptance of its harrowing dictates: it threatens us with our greatest fear, expulsion from our community. How many times must Sorrow be born? Can *any*thing be done? Or are we as a culture totally committed to the punishment and suffering of females? Does woman as scapegoat hold an irresistible appeal? Tess does do something: at last she murders the situation and, through death, escapes the world of man. Women want to share the world: they want men to take responsibility for its children. Hardy's poignant language invites us to ask if anything fundamental can be done.

I Stand Here Ironing invites the reader to grapple with the question in relation to the text. Little can be done, it seems, to prevent young female lives from being crippled and thwarted, yet perhaps something can be done to insure survival. There may be, as Tillie Olsen suggests, enough to live by. The so-called accidents of life determine, propel and grind us down: poverty, desertion, institutional indifference and cruelty, and a mother who loved but could not smile hardly constitute an auspicious beginning. A tentative triumph of the human spirit, however, suggests that the answer to the question, Can anything be done? may be more ambiguous in this tale than in any other in the section.

To Room Nineteen asks if a woman of fifty can see herself as young and unmarried, and "blossom from the root of what she had been twenty years before." Can anything be done by and for the woman who must be available to everyone because she is middle-class and middle-aged — a mother who has no identity apart from her relation to others? Susan longs for solitude, for people who have no claims on her because they do not know her. She tries to find privacy, peace and her*self*, and she suddenly finds she has lost her very essence somewhere within the confines of marriage, home and children. Susan finds suicide the only thing she can do. The frustration is magnified because Susan is in a position society considers privileged: yet this position erodes and destroys her. Susan has always played by the rules grounded in the sacrifice of the female. That the intelligent female capitulates and goes obligingly to the slaughter is difficult to accept. For the slaughter is slow, silent and relentless. It takes, Susan discovers, about twenty years.

Kamouraska details a double standard so profound that Elisabeth's biology is, to a great extent, her destiny. She is a young woman of spirit and passion. In every situation, however, her back is to the wall; in spite of her decisions, no real choices seem to have been available. Elisabeth did the best she could, but any real escape from the society that suffocates her seems as unlikely as a warm Quebec winter. Could anything that really mattered have been done? As Elisabeth reviews her life, bitterness and resentment become meat and drink to her. Life was hard for everyone in Kamouraska, but nothing was done to loose women from the double binds of dependency and determinism. To be female was to be captive.

The Scarlet Letter anticipates Virginia Woolf. Hester does not apologize: she does not explain. While she does not live out loud, her life has both colour and drama. To this extent she opts out of her society. The symbolism in this novel helps to illumine the complexity of moral issues: nothing is simply white, black or scarlet. Rather, all colours have both angelic and demonic sides. Adultery is rarely the public issue it once was but it identifies the society that considers woman a thing to be owned and punished. The complicity of men in such proceedings is most interestingly portrayed through Dimmesdale, who actually develops during this often static story. Pearl, the letter, the flowers, the physical beauty of Hester — all attest to personal strength vying with social and cultural powers. Hester, who never bows to society's censure yet participates in beautiful and useful ways, is an enigma transmitted through time and space with remarkable clarity. Can anything be done? Not much, in a punitive puritanical society devoted to stamping out lively impulse. However, an individual can nearly always interpret a situation in a way radically different from that of her society and, without compromising herself or her values, participate in that society although it lags far behind her in understanding and compassion. In this group of works, we have no examples of children's literature. "Can anything be done?" is a cry of despair, irony and tragedy: yet the very essence of childhood is hope. The vision presented in this chapter is the only one possible for many women in literature and life, but it is not primarily a vision of childhood.

TESS OF THE D'URBERVILLES
by
THOMAS HARDY

How it rained
When we worked at Flintcomb-Ash,
And could not stand upon the hill

Trimming swedes for the slicing-mill.
The wet washed through us — plash, plash, plash:
How it rained!

How it snowed
When we crossed from Flintcomb-Ash
To the Great Barn for drawing reed,
Since we could nowise chop a swede. —
Flakes in each doorway and casement-sash:
How it snowed!

How it shone
When we went from Flintcomb-Ash
To start at dairywork once more
In the laughing meads, with cows three-score,
And pails, and songs, and love — too rash:
How it shone![1]

...she becomes part and parcel of outdoor nature and is not merely
an object set down therein as at ordinary times. A field-man is a
personality afield; a field-woman is a portion of the field, she has
somehow lost her own margin, imbibed the essence of her
surrounding, and assimilated herself with it.[2]

There is probably no Victorian novelist who, more completely
than Hardy, embodies what contemporary structuralists and
post-structuralists would term the "mechanics of signification."
When Michael Riffaterre[3] asserts that it is impossible really to
read a story by paying close attention to the narrative and
skimming or skipping the description, he might have Hardy as
well as Dickens and Trollope in mind. Description in Hardy's
novels is an integral part of narration. The Vale of Blakemore is
"an engirdled and secluded region, for the most part untrodden
as yet by tourist or landscape painter." Tess, too, is virginal and in
danger of being trespassed upon. We will soon feel the devastating
and irrevocable effects of the Industrial Revolution as Hardy
portrays it. Village life and human perception are impinged upon
by what he recognizes as the evils of modernism — its technology,
its money, its religion and its ideas.

Description may be a particularly important aspect of narration
in works that have a female at the centre. Our racial memory

carries us back to earth mothers, field goddesses, good and evil
female fairies, our own mother's body, the female seed gatherers,
the priestesses of ancient days. Not only does identification with
her environment reveal Tess; it also reveals her attempts to live
and be distinct from it. She is in it, its product and its victim, but
not simply or consistently of it.

> Superstitions linger longest on these heavy soils. Having once
> been forest, at this shadowy time it seemed to assert something of
> its old character. The harts that had been hunted here, the witches
> that had been pricked and ducked, the green-spangled fairies that
> "wickered" at you as you passed.[4]

These influences are part of Tess's heritage, but Tess, who has
inherited her mother's physical loveliness, belongs to a new
world. "Between the mother . . . and the daughter . . . there was a
gap of two hundred years as ordinarily understood. When they
were together the Jacobean and Victorian ages were juxtaposed."[5]
"Tess had . . . some anachronistic D'Urberville current in her
blood that makes for spiritual exacerbation just as it makes her
cheeks paler, the teeth more regular, the red lips thinner than is
usual in the country-bred girl."[6] Anatomy is destiny — a
contemporary cry with historical traces and psychological roots
that go deep within us all. Typical metaphors for this determinism
are a cage, or, more seductively, an enclosed garden, from which
women try, often somewhat ambiguously, to escape. As Milton
reminds us in *Samson Agonistes*, we tend to choose bondage with
ease rather than strenuous liberty. Hardy provides us with signs
very early on that for Tess tragedy is inevitable.

Hardy's theme in *Tess of the D'Urbervilles* is ancient and, if there
is such an entity, universal as well. For "there was something
more to be said in fiction than had been said about the shaded side
of a well-known catastrophe."[7] The rural Victorian setting
provided by the Bard of Wessex distances the contemporary
reader, which is helpful to aesthetic and moral understanding. It
also prepares for the jolt of recognition that nothing really
changes. Finally we are brought up short by Hardy's insight that
when a married woman who has a lover kills her husband, she

does not really wish to kill the husband; she wishes to kill the situation.

There is certainly a contemporary ring here. While a woman rarely kills her husband, although she may fantasize about his early demise, there must be some kind of killing, however symbolic or ritualistic, to effect her release. Once domesticated, it is difficult to learn to be free, to dare, or to remember how to be wild.

> When Alec finds Tess working at Flintcomb Ash, he waits until she is totally exhausted by the threshing-machine before offering help. He makes Tess a "caged wretch": wild Nature become a household pet, its spirit suppressed until the opportunity for revenge presents itself. Angel believes Tess is a "domestic animal," perfectly at home at Talbothays. In seeing her as a "daughter of Nature," he forgets Nature's cruelty. Both men are ignorant of the laws of Necessity, aliens to the Natural order to which Tess belongs.[8]

If, in making moral decisions, people typically, though not always, experience inner conflict between the desire to do what they believe they ought to do and the desire to do something else,[9] it may be difficult to see Tess as a moral force. She is so much more acted upon than acting. Nevertheless, she is an exemplar of many women. Through Tess we can see clearly the constraints and social conditioning that are our legacy. Perhaps, more significantly, we can see in Tess the females of many contemporary cultures in which women experience virtually no self-determination. Within any group that heralds the birth of males with more fanfare than that of females, we see women doomed to male decision-making and policy-making. Wherever males are searching for "untried lips", so that they may own a woman, the tragedy of Tess is re-enacted.

Having said all this, there is an inevitability and inexorability about the story of Tess that makes her inner conflict less than that of women in apparently freer circumstances. Her innocence, her not knowing, is at the core. Tess even scolds her mother for not sharing with her the knowledge of good and evil through the vicarious experience of fiction.

How could I be expected to know? I was a child when I left this house four months ago. Why didn't you tell me there was danger in menfolk? Why didn't you warn me? Ladies know what to fend hands against, because they read novels that tell them of these tricks; but I never had the chance of learning in that way, and you did not help me.[10]

Considering Tess's abrupt descent into the world of experience, Hardy observes that "but for the world's opinion, those experiences would have been simply a liberal education."[11] Hardy is quite clear that Tess has committed a social sin only. Recognizing, in the first of many schizophrenic images of the book, that Tess will be cut off from herself by "an immeasurable social chasm,"[12] he rejects the convention that the seduction of the heroine was the "virtual ending to enterprises and hopes."[13] On the contrary, "Hardy treats this as the moment from which Tess's heroism begins."[14] The rape scene is not written, because what matters is its consequences: Tess's moral purity is not identified with her physical virginity. Real morality for Hardy is more profound, more personal, more political than any code of social manners. Tess becomes a paradigm for contemporary feminist thought that seeks to go beyond the separation of public and private morality.

How Tess copes becomes all-important. "Because of her resilience, adaptability and independence, she breaks free of the man who mastered her body, and faces the harsh reality she brings upon herself with dignity and courage, although alone."[15] "Let the truth be told," pleads Hardy, "women do as a rule live through such humiliations, and regain their spirits."[16]

If Tess's behaviour has a moral component, it is her innocence, the responsibility for which she places squarely and with some justification on her mother. This is the same innocence with which the contemporary world is rapidly losing patience and is exemplified by men who "know not what they do" in their attitudes towards and their treatment of women, and by women who are unaware of considering themselves to be secondary. Margaret Laurence labelled innocence the "eighth deadly sin."[17] Tess is described as a "mere vessel of emotion untinctured by experience"[18] and her situation is compared to the garden of Eden before the fall: "The garden in which the cottage stood was surrounded by a wall and could only be entered by a door."[19]

For Hardy, there exist many fallen worlds. Old families have fallen, their names and ways corrupted; the Industrial Revolution is a final expulsion from Eden. Tess's fall in the midst of all this tumbling is particularly ironic, as it is the conventional fall of the "fallen woman", yet it is free of moral taint. But, paradoxically, her very innocence is deviant behaviour, and unwittingly invites dire consequences. Our lost paradise is always haunting us with "the lively presence of its absence": Tess describes herself as an "apple" that is "blighted."[20] In her outburst to her mother, Tess acknowledges that both her innocence and Alec's experience, including his inability to comprehend innocence, created her present suffering. Nevertheless, we are left with the sinking feeling that her fate has been more in her stars than in herself.

The depiction of Tess's nocturnal walks during her pregnancy might be illuminating reading for abortion committees striving to understand what it really means to be pregnant and alone. Tess feels all Nature accusing her, social taboos being buttressed and reinforced by the elements themselves. For her, what they seemed, they were. Hardy explains to the reader that Tess's perception — that she is guilty, miserable and rejected by both the human and the natural worlds — misses the mark. Hardy portrays Tess as victim and the reader is likely to share this view, as even the egocentric Angel eventually does. Tess, however, never accepts herself or her situation. Instead she experiences the alienation of the ages, of simply being female, desired and therefore guilty.

Hardy sees an innate affinity between the female and nature. After Sorrow is born, Tess goes to work in the fields, a place, like Tess, of fertility and naturalness. "The earth is primarily not a metaphor but a real thing"[21] and for Hardy it so often obstructs human desire and purpose. When Tess leaves the fields to nurse the child, she is a picturesque madonna reddened only slightly by her consciousness of social disapproval. Yet Hardy again distinguishes between Tess's perception and that of society. She experiences hurt and exclusion; society, traditionally harder on pregnancy than on motherhood, becomes indifferent.

> She might have seen that what had bowed her head so profoundly — the thought of the world's concern at her situation — was founded on an illusion. She was not an existence, an experience, a passion, a "structure of sensations" to anybody but herself. To all humankind besides, Tess was only a passing thought.[22]

Society's lack of concern for its individuals pales before nature's colossal indifference to the puny human race that scrambles about on the earth's surface.

> Whatever its consequences, time would close over them; they would all in a few years be as if they had never been, and she herself grassed down and forgotten. Meanwhile the trees were just as green as before; the birds sang and the sun shone as clearly now as ever. The familiar surroundings had not darkened because of her grief, nor sickened because of her pain.[23]

As Tess cannot find comfort in nature, she seeks it in the certainty of her own present life and of her "grassing down." Tess wonders which day of the year is that important but unknown day of her death, "a day which lay sly and unseen among all other days of the year, giving no sign or sound when she actually passed over it; but not the less surely there."[24]

Tess remains a divided soul, torn between her conventional aspect and "the natural side of her which knew no social law." Alternately she is passionate and indifferent to her child, vacillating between nature and society as she perceives them. Tess is very young, but she is seen as a maternal figure. Her relation to her siblings is described as "deputy-maternal." Later, the child becomes mother of the woman when she exchanges roles with Joan, "an additional one, and that not the eldest, to her own long line of waiters upon Providence."[25] Motherhood makes Tess a hero in her efforts to save the child, through baptism, from eternal damnation.

Perhaps because she is so much the vehicle of Hardy's ideas and more often the object than the subject of the action, we are somewhat baffled by Tess. Her morality, unlike Hester's, is conventional; her beliefs are shot through with superstition; and her motivation, unconcerned with ultimate goals, is immediate and short-sighted. Like so many women in life and in fiction, she does what she is told. We must, however, remember the complicated system of rewards which still exists for the obedient female. In many countries and cultures, the reward for female submission is continued physical survival. Our own family and school systems, too, reward the obedient little girl, and in many institutionalized religions she may be asked when she grows up to make a marriage vow of obedience to her husband. If we scoff at this vow as only a form, we trivialize the potency of language.

Tess takes the line of least resistance and follows the dictates of authority figures. Her relationships with men are largely passive, although not entirely so. Part of Tess's suffering is precipitated by "her father's vainglorious attempts to reclaim his former aristocratic ancestry and the distant D'Urberville history."[26] After Angel's proposal comes a process of soul-searching that becomes one of submission. Obedience to her mother, a most unreliable authority, strongly influences her decision to reveal her past to Angel.* Full revelation of one's past life, sexual or otherwise, may no longer be a moral condition for marriage; but in Tess's world, such revelations by women were expected.

When Angel, the minister's son who plays the harp and is hidden in an apple orchard, is chagrined, Tess offers him complete obedience, even unto death: "I will obey you like your wretched slave, even if it is to lie down and die."[27] Later Tess allows Alec to persuade her that Angel will not return. The only action Tess performs without any external persuasion is Alec's murder, yet even here, we should not underestimate the influence of Angel's suggestion that, "If he were dead it might be different."[28] Tess's repeated failure to act upon her own better judgement may reflect Hardy's definition of morality, which is eventually accepted by Angel: "Who was the moral man? Still more pertinently, who was the moral woman? The beauty or ugliness of a character lay not only in its achievements, but in its aims and impulses; its true history lay, not among things done,

* Hardy's *A Pair of Blue Eyes* depicts a similar moral dilemma.

but among things willed."[29] Such morality, with its emphasis upon motive, will and impulse may seem to be personal and private, and thus different from public and social morality, which focuses on behaviour and action. Yet so-called private morality quickly merges with public morality. There seems no defense against the seduction of Tess, yet Alec's murder, which results, is a matter worthy of public hanging. Can any moral action really be the exclusive preserve of the individual without impinging upon the public?

Finite and unimaginative creatures that we are, our greatest concern is usually for those close to us. In matters of principle and in politics, however, the boundaries of our concern need know no limits. Tess may have been only a passing thought to others, but even in her tiny, enclosed world her decisions and her tragedy affect them. Tess's morality is essentially a morality of the helpless, of the oppressed, whose cardinal virtue is endurance. "Patience, that blending of moral courage with physical timidity, was no longer a minor feature in Mrs. Angel Clare; and it sustained her."[30] Men are expected to do, women simply to be. Tess, in this context, is a pure woman, long-suffering, consistently loving good and disliking evil. Angel Clare, who is neither angelic nor clear in thought and action, does revise his morality through an understanding of the pathos of life. "While tragedy may massacre an entire cast, pathos is usually concentrated on a single character...and is increased by the inarticulateness of the victim. Pathos is a queer, ghoulish emotion, and some failure of expression, real or simulated, seems peculiar to it."[31]

Tess is certainly an inarticulate victim: events conspire to thwart her attempt to tell Angel of her "fallen" state. Clare, from whom Tess's experience is as far removed as her innocence had been from Alec, refuses to listen. The gossip of Tess's companions increases her isolation and effectively gags her: "Yes, there was the pain of it. This question of a woman telling her story — the heaviest of crosses to herself — seemed but amusement to others. It was as if people should laugh at martyrdom."[32] The insistence of Tess's mother, the encouragement of the other milkmaids, and, finally, even the attic carpet conspire against Tess's revelation. "Tess and all the other Talbothay milkmaids are reduced to the same helpless misery by their feelings for Angel. All differences between them, all their attempts at individuality, are 'abstracted by the passion, and each is but a portion of one organism called sex'."[33] Tess does not confess to Angel: she does not tell him about the nocturnal walk, the revelation of which, he admits, might have changed everything. Her attempt to contact Angel's father is aborted. She does not communicate with Angel while he is away, in obedience to an order long ago given and forgotten. Her one plea for help must be corroborated by the letter from Marion and Izz.

There is no denying her functional inarticulateness. How often does she manage to communicate her real feelings? In her first conversation with Clare, "she was expressing in her own native phrases — assisted a little by her Sixth Standard training — feelings that might almost have been called those of the age — the ache of modernism."[34] As her teacher, Angel finds her not only quick, but thorough: "Her natural quickness and admiration for him having led her to pick up his vocabulary, his accent, and fragments of his knowledge to a surprising extent."[35] Tess's memory is tenacious. Yet when she later teaches Alec, reciting some of Clare's wisdom with perfect accuracy, she admits that she does not really understand it. She has a simple and complete faith in Angel's power to support his confessed beliefs.

We do hear Angel's wisdom recited to Alec; it is subordinated to its effects. Tess's confession to Angel on their wedding night is similarly implied, but Alec's murder is dealt with head on. Tess confesses without hesitation and Angel accepts with some doubts but no questions. Tess speaks for herself while the author busies himself with a rather morbid account of Alec's body.

Although slight attention is paid to Tess's words, much is made of her voice — its sound and the beautiful aperture from which it issues. Clare notices Tess for the first time when he is struck by the "flutey" sound of her voice, which follows him to his refuge in his parents' house, "cooing" at him in the darkness. When Tess is reciting the rite of baptism over her dying infant, the words are not her own but she utters them "boldly and triumphantly in the stopt-diapason note which her voice acquired when her heart was in her speech, and which will never be forgotten by those who knew her."[36]

Tess's disembodied voice is more music than speech, in ironic contrast with her failure of expression. The emphasis throughout the novel on sound and sight rather than dialogue and action defines Tess's function. She is a presence: she may not have a heroine's power of action, but she has vibrant life. Even the high-minded Angel appreciates the life in Tess. Tess's eloquence is physical rather than verbal. Her powerful physicality is a source of sexual temptation to Alec and Angel, both of whom describe Tess's mouth as "maddening." Alec's evangelical passion dissolves in his rekindled lust: "Surely there never was such a maddening mouth since Eve's....You temptress, Tess, you dear damned witch of Babylon — I could not resist you as soon as I met you again."[37]

The reference to Eve is certainly not new to us in connection with Tess and her garden. The "witch of Babylon," however, describes not Tess but the effect she has on Alec. Tess is a temptress to Angel as well. Upon his return to the dairy, a veritable garden of Eden, the fallen Angel discovers the serpent: "She was yawning, and he saw the red interior of her mouth as if it had been a snake's. She had stretched one arm so high above her coiled up cable of hair that he could see its satin delicateness above the sunburn....She regarded him as Eve at her second waking might have regarded Adam."[38] The seduction by Alec and, to a lesser extent, by Angel as well, are not among things willed. It is one thing to dissociate oneself from one's actions when one is raped or forced, but quite another to separate oneself from one's corporeal self. This is, nevertheless, what seems to happen when Tess returns to Alec. Angel becomes uneasily aware of her state when he meets Tess in Sandbourne: "His original Tess had spiritually ceased to recognize the body before him as hers — allowing it to drift, like a corpse upon a current, in a direction dissociated from its living will."[39]

Angel blames Alec's murder on a mental aberration; yet Tess is not ignorant of the consequences. She knows them full well and is resolved to accept all to gain Angel's forgiveness. If she is absent from her body when Angel meets her, she returns to it rapidly once Alec is dead. Alec's death, her only willed action, is a ritual expiation of the past.

> It is a kind of suicide, aligning her with all the great tragic heroines prepared to die to save or avenge their honour. Her murder gives her private experience public significance, exposing her to public judgement and revenge. Her death itself is a ritual execution, [like her] sleep upon the altar, where the sun's rays strike her.[40]

Moral justification for the murder of Alec may not be within social law: seducer he may be, but he was certainly kinder to Tess's family than Angel was. While Angel, with his new-found moral enlightenment, concludes that her love for him has "extinguished moral sense altogether," we may understand it in terms of Ursula LeGuin's depiction of moral elements in fairy tale and dream:

> Under no conditions can we say that it is morally right or ethically virtuous to push an old lady into a baking oven. But, under the conditions of fairy tale, we can say with perfect conviction that it may be appropriate to do so....The hero or heroine is the one who sees what is appropriate to be done, because he or she sees the whole which is greater than either evil or good.[41]

This certainty of the appropriate thing that can be done is shared by Tess:

> But I don't blame you; only Angel, will you forgive my sin against you, now I have killed him? I thought as I ran along that you would be sure to forgive me now I have done that. It came to me as a shining light that I should get you back that way.[42]

The dreamlike quality of the story from the point at which Tess and Angel meet again until she is taken away to the gallows supports the sense of expiation and ritual killing. While the final scenes of the book add to our sense of inevitability and hopelessness, they do not obscure Tess's sexual tragedy. "Generalizations on the nature of women are at the root of sexual tragedy....Men and women are unable to regard themselves as anything but separate species."[43] Because Angel sees Tess as a being apart, he sets higher standards for her than for himself, cruelly insisting that she conform to his ideal. He cannot see their crimes as equal. Tess must suffer the injustice of man-made law.

Can anything be done? The sombre notes and the inexorable movement of the novel suggest a determinism from which there is no escape. What Tess does may be all she can do; the ending is an existential one. Yet, in a sense, we have the happiest of tragic endings possible: the victim, finally, through her own volition, controls a part of life.

Can anything be done on a more profound level to ameliorate societal forces that insist that a man shall be guiltless while a woman shall bear her iniquity? As Hardy's novel reveals, sexual biases and fears are deep within us all. The carefully considered murder of these biases and fears might yet set us free. Much questioning and reflection is necessary; no child should be left innocent by home or school, as Tess was.

For the reader who craves distinct villains and victims this novel will provide constant frustration. For the reader intrigued by the tension between appearance and reality and the primitive subtleties of motivation, intentions and action between the sexes, *Tess of the D'Urbervilles* remains a fertile source for speculation and moral inquiry.

I STAND IRONING
by
TILLIE OLSEN

In Tillie Olsen's story, we find the most positive response of any of these texts to the question, can anything be done? Its human answer seems to be that, while not enough good can be done and much that is unfortunate and evil will be done, what small things *can* be done are always worth the effort. This is a mother-and-daughter story, less violent, less complex certainly, but in some ways reminiscent of that of Morag and Pique in *The Diviners*. Like

Morag, the mother who stands ironing knows she doesn't know much about her daughter. She says to her unidentified interrogator, "You think because I am her mother I have a key, or that in some way you could use me as a key? She has lived for nineteen years. There is all that life that has happened outside me, beyond me." Then the mother remembers her "beautiful baby, a miracle," in a poignant reminiscence of joy and guilt, pride and anxiety. The mother was nineteen, Emily's age, when her daughter was born. The father "could no longer endure sharing want" with his family and decamped, leaving mother and daughter to manage. Can anything be done?

Many things that were done should not have been done — Emily's nursery school employed sadistic teachers; the convalescent home in the country did not allow children to keep cards and letters from home. The mother could not, as an old man advised her, smile at Emily. Later, when she had emotional and financial security, she was able to smile at Emily's brothers and sisters; but Emily, while passionately loved, was loved by a tired, anxious woman unable to smile. Tillie Olsen captures the problems of the single mother, of the working, and overworked, poor. When women are too tired to smile at children they passionately love, something is wrong with their society. Emily and her mother hang on, but at a crucial time they are abandoned by husband and father and by an uncaring system. There is a great deal of rhetoric declaring children to be our greatest resource. Do we really believe it? "Emily fretted about her appearance, thin and dark and foreign-looking at a time when every little girl was supposed to look a chubby, blonde replica of Shirley Temple." Beauty may be in the eye of the beholder, but it takes a hardy individual to see beauty where one has not been conditioned to find it. While all people are judged by their appearances, the pressures on female children are stronger than on males. Children and adolescents are conformists, and it is helpful to see how rigid and how cruel the dictates of fickle fashion can be.

School was a worry to her. She was not glib in a world where glibness and quickness were easily confused with ability to learn. To her overworked and exasperated teachers she was an over conscientious "slow learner" who kept trying to catch up and was absent entirely too often.[44]

Institutions, too, are inadequate. Something might be done about inhuman convalescent homes and overworked teachers and stereotyped notions of the learner. Yet such is human resilience that in spite of, or partly because of, her deprivations, the girl who didn't receive or give smiles, while still fragile and permanently maimed, becomes a comedian, able to make others laugh. Her mother concludes: "She has much to her and probably little will come of it. She is a child of her age, of depression, of war, of fear."[45]

Tess, too, is a child of her age. So is Hester. So is Elisabeth. So are we all. The accident of birth, the age, the institutions, the economics of our time determine and condition us. Can anything be done? Perhaps something right and good and even beautiful was done by the mother who stands ironing: "Let her be. So all that is in her will not bloom — but in how many does it? There is still enough left to live by."[46] Perhaps we can live by what we have, even though all that is in us will never bloom. This is a difficult position, resignation to a fallen world and compromise with inadequate people and systems; yet within it, perhaps, there is just enough hope to live by.

TO ROOM NINETEEN
by
DORIS LESSING

Doris Lessing has been hailed by critics for breaking new ground both in content and technique. Susan, the central figure in *To Room Nineteen*, is caught between ideologies. One holds that the exercise of intelligence in one's personal life will ensure that all goes well; one will be able to handle problems sensibly without disrupting the status quo. Lessing begins her tale by remarking, "This is a story, I suppose, about a failure in intelligence: the Rawlings's marriage was grounded in intelligence." The Rawlings were sensible; both had well-paid jobs; they married in their well-seasoned late twenties and, Lessing reminds us, did fall in love.

> It was typical of this couple that they had a son first, then a daughter, then twins, son and daughter. Everything right, appropriate, and what everyone would wish for, if they could choose. But people did feel these two had chosen; this balanced and sensible family was no more than what was due to them because of their infallible sense for choosing right.[47]

There are many biblical allusions to serpent, garden and devil. The garden is the place Susan eventually fears to enter alone, because there she meets the horror, the fact that her life has no centre, but is defined, as are the lives of so many women, by her relationships. There is no place to hide — from Matthew, Fred, Mrs. Parkes, Mrs. Townsend or a devil. City (Mrs. Townsend) and suburb (Mrs. Parkes) alike threaten her need to be alone. Children, women and men consider it their inalienable right to make demands on her: the room arranged for Susan soon becomes a family room — a drop-in centre. When the children are all at school, there is still the "daily woman," whom Lessing explains is a "server," but a server needs somebody to serve. Susan's holiday in the wild Welsh countryside is so punctuated by calls from servants and family that she is on a short leash of telephone wire. Small wonder that "the devils of exasperation dance in the blood"[48] of the Susans of life and literature.

Everyone is fair and considerate; yet, in order to preserve appearances and maintain order, lies must be told. When the story has ended, although it is not yet over, Matthew believes and hopes that Susan has taken a lover; he suggests that they join him and his mistress in a civilized foursome. "We could all meet for lunch, I mean, it's ridiculous, you sneaking off to filthy hotels, and me staying late at the office and all the lies everyone has to tell." Yet the very lies that break one moral contract often help to fulfill another — that of kindness and consideration. This theme repeats itself in almost all of the tales we tell.

"The observance of a magnificent form," as Isabel Archer Osmond called her allegiance to her married state, is something Susan tries to maintain.

So what did it matter that they felt dry, flat? People like themselves, fed on a hundred books (psychological, anthro-pological, sociological) could scarcely be unprepared for the dry, controlled wistfulness which is the distinguishing mark of the intelligent marriage. These two unsurprised, turned toward each other with even more courtesy and gentle love: this was life, that two people, no matter how carefully chosen, could not be everything to each other.

Susan is also ashamed of the word "bondage" when she thinks about human bondage. "And that word bondage — why had she used it? She had never felt marriage, or the children, as bondage."[49] Susan longs for a room of her own.

Susan is weighed down with the existential guilt felt by so many women and men who have no control over their lives. She becomes "determined to arrange her life, no matter what it cost, so that she could have...solitude more often. An absolute solitude where no one knew her or cared about her."[50] In Room Nineteen, Susan is able to lean on the sill and look into the street "loving the men and women because she did not know them."

Can anything be done? Can a woman past the middle of her life, who has devoted herself to the contentment of her husband, the management of her home and the nurturing and launching of children for more than twenty years, find her earlier talents, her long-lapsed interests? Is it possible to reach back across the years and recapture her former self? Can she ever again have an identity unencumbered by appendages? The questions assail Susan in rapid succession. Can the "essential Susan" be put in cold storage? What is this "essential Susan"? Can women in families in the late twentieth century be all things to all people all the time and not lose their essential selves? The determinism of biology, sociology, social norms and morality is difficult to transcend or to escape, partly, at least, because it is so difficult to see. Many women like Susan who have everything find that everything is too much. Their essential selves are submerged in everything, and it is often impossible for them to re-emerge. Many, like Susan, kill themselves: many more live lives of drug-addicted depression. For beneath the institutions of marriage and family is a deeper moral issue that Lessing is inviting us to unearth. Can anything be done?

KAMOURASKA
by
ANNE HEBERT

Elisabeth d'Aulnières recalls her life as she sits by her second husband's death-bed. As she offers him water, which he trusts her too little to accept, the reader overhears her story. Elisabeth is a victim — of her beauty, her sexuality, her passion, her respectable relatives, her self-centred husbands, her lover and her society. Again and again the reader pleads, "Can anything be done?"

There is no escape for a young girl from the smothering and demanding respectability of a home in which a mother and a gaggle of proper aunts dictate and control her every move. A real home, a real life of her own do not seem to be genuine options. She has spirit and passion but, in the end, she is overwhelmed.

Elisabeth enjoys hunting — not a generally accepted female pastime — and the squire of Kamouraska, Antoine Tassey, admires her skill as well as her beauty. As a liberator, he is a pretty poor specimen: a bully, a drunk, a depressive and generally licentious man who abuses and beats her. Her choice of men, like all her choices, is extremely narrow. Small wonder, given her repressed anger and her mother-in-law's urgings to accept a "woman's lot" at the hand of her husband, that this passionate woman fastens upon her husband's former class-mate, George Nelson, now the local doctor and, therefore, the only man with whom she is permitted to be alone. Escape, for Elisabeth, as for so many women, means only a change of captors. No real liberty is possible.

The aunts, to their credit, give her protection along with confinement. When she has endured public censure as the probable murderer of her husband, whom she certainly wished dead, and her lover has fled back to the United States, another rescue takes place. Yet this rescue, effected by Jerome Rolland, "so round and plump, so small in the enormous dressing gown . . .

with its checks and its fancy buttons," is condemnation to another tyranny and the bearing of many babies. "We go on living as if nothing at all had happened, then suddenly the poison deep in our hearts comes rising up to the surface."[51]

The entire tale is told in flashbacks as Elisabeth remembers with bitterness and regret a life held in thrall by others. In keeping with the irony and secrecy of her story, even her tears are misinterpreted. When she cries in anguish over the loss of her time, her energy, her passion, her life, someone whispers, "Just look how Madame loves Monsieur. You see, she's crying." It is at the altars of appearance and respectability that Elisabeth must be sacrificed again and again.

Life is difficult for all the inhabitants of Kamouraska, but what power there is resides primarily in men who are advantaged in physical, sexual and social mobility and, of course, economic power. Antoine can squander the family substance upon riotous living while Elisabeth scrounges food for their children. It is ironic that she is a good shot and enjoys hunting, when she is herself always preyed upon. The enormity of her resentment and bitterness, of her dependence and loss, suffuse the rhetoric Elisabeth summons to tell her tale.

THE SCARLET LETTER
by
NATHANIEL HAWTHORNE

The Scarlet Letter is a hardy perennial among the flowers of American literature, and, indeed, flowers and weeds abound in its imagery. It takes place in a world in which woman is property, although often cherished property. The novel is symbolic and must be studied as such. As a societal issue, adultery may be passé, but it still elicits venom and revenge — occasionally even murder — in individuals. The notion of trespassing on private property is a crucial one. Woman is property; and the entire community conspires to restrict and confine her freedom and latitude. According to New England Puritanism, natural women and men were corrupt and energy was constantly expended to overcome one's natural self. Law and religion were used conjointly to subdue *natural* human tendencies and predilections.

Hester is the symbol of natural beauty who shuns the drab and dreary Puritan ethic and is associated with colour and sunshine. She does not so much contravene the established order; rather, she chooses to live outside its strictures.

Chillingworth, as his name implies, is a cold fish. His touchstone is the intellect, but when he seeks revenge he violates even his own intellectual nature; consumed with the desire for revenge, he dies when he no longer has an object to hate. Dimmesdale is more concerned with things spiritual. When he ascends the scaffold, confesses and dies, he at last becomes admirable.

Hester develops into the ideal of saintly living, spending her days in generous service to others. She makes amends but never repents. The reader is not likely to question the authenticity of Hester's later life, but serious questions may be raised about whether she sinned. Were her violations simply against the social code of her time and place, or was there a moral dimension as well? How free are we to go against the grain of society's prevailing moral system if our decision inescapably involves others? Is it ever possible to act morally without implicating others, particularly in a society like that of Hester, that increasingly merges private and public? (As one grade-ten boy, supposedly suffering from reading problems, sagely and succinctly put it, "That lady weren't no whore!") Hester is ambiguous: in her relation to nature she differs from not only Chillingworth and Dimmesdale, but also, of course, from the other women of the town.

Pearl, Hester's daughter, is identified with beauty and nature. It seemed, Hawthorne observes, that she had not been made at all, "but plucked by her mother off the bush of wild roses that grew by the prison door." At the governor's house, Pearl demands a rose. She throws flowers at her mother and they nearly always hit the letter "A" embroidered in scarlet on her mother's bosom. She has a natural affinity to the animals: she plucks out weeds pretending they are the Puritan children, and sees the pine trees, aged, black and solemn, as the Puritan elders. Pearl comes close to being an abstraction, but symbolically she expresses hope. The author gives us assurance of Pearl's future well-being, indicating that he is not in favour of the sins, if such they be, of the parents being visited upon the second generation, let alone the third or fourth.

The Scarlet Letter, narrowly considered, provides us with a symbol to dispose of those who would not sympathize with Hester in her hatred of Chillingworth and her love for Dimmesdale. She and her beautifully embroidered scarlet letter have become a metaphor in modern culture. Her continuing life, albeit narrowly circumscribed, represents a victory; her husband and lover die from revenge and guilt, respectively. Hawthorne condemns the lack of charity in Puritan New England with a force unequalled except in Corinthians 13. Today there are places where women are still spurned and even killed for adultery. The wider issue Hawthorne raises, however, is that of a community's treatment of those who violate its codes. In a multi-cultured society, groups are divided as to which issues are strictly social and which involve moral elements. Tolerance of the divisions is healing and consensus, while it cannot be achieved, is worth striving for. *The Scarlet Letter* shows us what *not* to do. To isolate one person, to create a scapegoat, to exclude an individual from the group may violate not only sound reason but also human charity. Whenever a society victimizes one of its members, it diminishes itself.

▲

CHAPTER FOUR

GRACE
UNDER PRESSURE

I N THE CONTEMPORARY WORLD, grace under any circumstances is in short supply. When, for whatever reasons, we find ourselves under pressure, we may have little room to manoeuvre, but we always have some options. We can fall apart, we can rail against whatever gods there be or we can do what we believe we must without rancour, malice or martyrdom. With good grace. The "grace under pressure" of this chapter is a subtle affair, neither stoic endurance nor mindless capitulation.* Grace may involve weakness or indecision, but such is rarely the case. More often it comes as a mature response to the recognition of one's extremity, a resolve to behave in a certain way. It may seem to do outrage to the female struggle against the pressures of her sex, time, age, place and society. This is for the reader to determine. The psychological and sociological benefits of grace can be endlessly debated.

In Henry James's *Portrait of a Lady*, Isabel admits her own complicity in the wretched marriage she has contracted. She married before all the world but she pretended to Osmond that there was less of her than there really was. She exercises her will in deciding to relinquish freedom and to be honour-bound by a "magnificent form." To trivialize Isabel's motivation as un-fashionable and out-of-date would be unfair. To see her as no more than the victim of a fortune-hunter, however, would be simplistic.

---

*Grace from other contexts is always possible so it should be stressed at the outset that no attempt is being made to invoke the macho meanings of Hemingway.

Lucy Maud Montgomery's *Anne of Green Gables* is rediscovered by each generation. Anne decides to cut short her intellectual growth for the sake of others, for conformity and, perhaps, for herself. There is nothing of the martyr in Anne; if she is a victim, she is a joyful and willing one, and certainly is unaware of being one. A lively mind and imagination she has always had: a loving family is a new experience. Her new grace may issue from internalized societal expectations, but her gracious caring for others far exceeds conventional demands. While it is possible that choice for Anne, as for many young women, is largely illusory, she shoulders her responsibility with goodwill and cheer.

Somerset Maugham's *The Promise* considers the sanctity of the given word in a mirror image of *Portrait of a Lady*. Here the promise given by a beautiful and accomplished older woman to a younger and devoted man is "to release him and let him love again" should he so desire. In his intention to marry a more socially acceptable companion, he may seem dull and shallow. No matter: Lady Elizabeth Vermont loves him, yet summons the strength to behave with grace and style when pressure is applied. To abstain from putting pressure on others may be the ultimate act of grace.

In *To the Lighthouse*, Virginia Woolf provides us with our most complex example of grace under pressure. Only *Portrait of a Lady* rivals its protracted tensions, silent pressures and infinite interpretive possibilities. In her living and dying, Mrs. Ramsay is full of grace. In her life, she exercises amazing grace under the onslaughts of demanding children, her husband and an assortment of hangers-on. Mrs. Ramsay does not appear to suffer as Susan of *To Room Nineteen* does in her late middle years. Is this because much of Mrs. Ramsay's grace emanates from a power many women never experience? She steers and manipulates, using her sexual and maternal powers to sustain all who surround her. Lily, the unmarried artist, demonstrates a different grace under very different pressures. Mrs. Ramsay, as sexual and nurturing woman, has reached her zenith. Her children are coupling and she presides over the fragmented household magnificently. However, is she needed any longer except as a presence — a disembodied spirit? There are hints in *To The Lighthouse* that the artist may be the one female not bound by the biological cycle to give meaning to her life.

Lyn Cook's *A Treasure for Tony*, a story about growing up in Canada, brings together age-old responses and contemporary settings in a blend just outside time and space. The pressures of today — racism, urban sprawl, marriage breakdown — are met by the young Antonia with the grace we may associate with earlier times. She has been blessed by love and emotional stability and she is a good advertisement for their influence upon the human spirit. She is not a pushover: she is determined, strong-willed and highly imaginative. She is not, however, willing to push others over. Her grace consists in accepting defeat, ridicule, loss of a home and a loved one with resilience and creativity.

All the females in this section have strong appeal, yet there is an underlying moral dilemma that grates and discomfits. When characters are able to resolve, even temporarily, the conflicting needs of others and self with a gracious spirit, it is likely to involve many personal sacrifices, and women know they have sacrificed too much for too long. However, the narcissistic, egocentric life is not an ideal for most people of sensitivity. Concern for others and freedom for oneself clash throughout this section, and stories of this conflict show the consequences of pain and choice to be unavoidable. When the clash is resolved with grace, certainty, calm and even at times euphoria may result.

PORTRAIT OF A LADY
by
HENRY JAMES

Isabel Archer was, of his three favourite heroines, the one James liked best: she is certainly the most popular among contemporary readers. Cynthia Ozick, writing in 1986, observes that "mysteriously, with the passing of each new decade, James becomes more and more our contemporary — it is as if our own sensibilities are only just catching up with his. We can recognize him now as a powerful symbolist of the psyche, one of the supreme literary innovators of consciousness."[1]

The tales of Henry James are proof that the human imagination can transcend gender. His understanding of the feminine mystique is universally acknowledged. Virginia Woolf believed that there was a specifically feminine mode of writing; however, as Terry Eagleton points out: "Some feminists have sharply rejected this theory, fearing that it simply reinvents some 'female essence' of a non-cultural kind, and perhaps also suspecting that it may be no more than a high-falutin version of the sexist view that women babble."[2] At the very least, however, Henry James is a writer with whom feminist literary theory must reckon, for he probes and depicts female consciousness and motivation with uncanny insight and clarity.

Many social historians have examined the chasm separating the male, downtown world of business and professions from the female, uptown world of the arts and social graces. Such a divide seems to have been the law of middle-class life in North America at the turn of the century. The American girl was supposed to supply, as James put it in the novel, "all the grace and all the interest that wasn't the mere interest on the money."

Grace is used in this chapter in a secular sense. However, in *Portrait of a Lady* there are echoes of its theological context — something given or received although it is neither earned nor deserved. For Isabel, grace means renunciation of freedom without martyrdom. When we meet Isabel she is "full of grace." However, it is only near the end of the novel that she is able to bestow grace upon those who have mightily wronged her.

In Isabel a vital democracy co-exists with a sense that she is special: Isabel cannot be like her unimaginative sisters. She sees herself slated for some grander destiny. We are told that Isabel possesses a finer mind than most of the persons among whom her lot was cast. Isabel's credo was simple, but subject to the dangers of inconsistency. "It was wrong to be mean, to be jealous, to be false, to be cruel."[3] Certain ethical problems had already plagued her: "What should one do with the misery of the world in a scheme of the agreeable for one's self?"[4]

The high moral principles to which Isabel is so wholeheartedly committed are in part a result of her American temperament and training; and they never really desert her. "She had had everything a girl could have: kindness, admiration, bonbons, bouquets, the sense of exclusion from none of the privileges of the world she lived in, abundant opportunity for dancing, plenty of new dresses, the London 'Spectator,' the latest publications, the music of Gounod, the poetry of Browning and the prose of George Eliot."[5] Admittedly, she had not experienced any "sense of exclusion from the privileges of the world she lived in," but "everything a girl could have" in her American world hardly prepared her for an older, more complex civilization where "kindness, admiration, bonbons and bouquets" may be closely related to opportunism.

Isabel is refreshing in her initial ability to say no to "suitable" suitors. She refuses the American Caspar Goodwood and — to the surprise and interest of her cousin, Ralph — the English peer, Lord Warburton. Among Isabel's many theories are rather definite ones concerning marriage. She felt, in general, that it was vulgar to think too much about it, and in particular, that one could be happy without a male companion: "I don't want to begin life by marrying. There are other things a woman can do." She is merely amused at the idea of being inspired to noble thoughts or actions by the men of her acquaintance. Nevertheless, sexual power absorbed her. At the time of her farewell to Goodwood, we are informed that "she felt each thing in his hard manhood." As Brownstein remarks, "this is a marvel of tactful specificity."[6] Like her namesake, Isabella in *Measure for Measure*, Isabel contemplates her own virtue.

While Isabel does not view marriage in quite the Shavian manner, she does fear its power to confine and inhibit: "The greatest sacrifice in marriage is the sacrifice of the adventurous attitude toward life: the being settled. Those who are born tired may crave for settlement; but to fresher and stronger spirits it is a form of suicide."[7] Isabel certainly will not surrender to marriage unless she considers someone worthy.

For Isabel had deeper fears regarding marriage — fears, as yet abstract, based on a vague recognition of her own tremendous capacity for commitment. "Deep in her soul — it was the deepest thing there — lay a belief that if a certain light should dawn she could give herself completely; but this image, on the whole, was too formidable to be attractive."[8]

Although Isabel is unsure of just why she rejects Lord Warburton, she is quite aware of what she has forfeited by her refusal: "the peace, the kindness, the honour, the possessions, a deep security and a great seclusion." Not long after her arrival at Gardencourt Isabel tells Ralph: "It's not absolutely necessary to suffer; we were not made for that."[9] Yet, by the time Lord Warburton discusses marriage, she believes she cannot escape unhappiness. When he accuses her of being overly enamoured of misery, Isabel candidly replies: "It comes over me every now and then that I can never be happy in any extraordinary way; not by turning away, by separating myself."[10]

Isabel refuses Warburton, not for his lack of good nature or good will, but for his lack of imagination. "Imagination" in James is always future oriented; it is a desire to achieve more than could be had by accepting what organized society considers pre-eminently valuable. "I don't need the aid of a clever man to teach me how to live, I can find it out for myself."[11] Isabel clings fiercely to her personal independence, although she admits that she may become "very sick" of it: "I try to judge things for myself; to judge wrong I think more honourable than not to judge at all. I don't wish to be a mere sheep in a flock; I wish to choose my fate, and know something of human affairs beyond what other people think it compatible with propriety to tell me."[12]

Lord Warburton feared "that remarkable mind". Isabel, too, is afraid of her mind. When she is analyzing the failure of her marriage she sees as not the least cause the fact that she had a mind of her own and a certain way of looking at life which Osmond took as a personal offence. Isabel is proof that the examined life, worth living or not, is often a torture.

To attempt, as men are encouraged to do, to be both good and clever elicits admiration from the Ralph Touchetts of the world, but they are a rare breed, as Isabel learns to her sorrow. Those females in fiction who follow Isabel will fight more vigorously and certainly more vociferously for their place in moral, intellectual and aesthetic suns, but none will cling more staunchly to her right to a certain way of seeing things than the Isabel Archer of 1881.

Among the "wheels to the coach," as James calls the characters who surround Isabel, none is more influential than Serena Merle. Her irresistible suavity masks a monster. She is to Isabel (another motherless young woman of fiction) an evil step-mother — "the smooth, white Madame Merle...Mother Earth perverted."[13] We are both attracted and repulsed by the Merle perfection and excessive cultivation. Gradually, however, we recoil from her infallibility, in everything from punctuality to paintings as she manipulates Isabel. Her overriding principle that the end justifies the means is apparent in her attitude towards marriage. When Isabel denies that she would care about the kind of house her supposed husband might own, Madame Merle replies:

> That's very crude of you....What shall we call our "self"? Where does it begin? Where does it end? It overflows into everything that belongs to us — and then it flows back again. I know a large part of myself is the clothes I choose to wear. One's self — for other people — is one's expression of one's self;...one's house, one's furniture, one's garments, the books one reads, the company one keeps.[14]
>
> Isabel responds: "I don't know whether I succeed in expressing myself, but I know that nothing else expresses me. Nothing that belongs to me is in any measure of me; everything's on the contrary a limit, a barrier, and a perfectly arbitrary one."[15]

Since Madame Merle is essentially evil and Isabel virtuous, we may be tempted to dismiss Madame Merle's position. But a careful reading of the text calls into serious question such over-simplification. However, when Osmond hypocritically describes the soul as immutable, Madame Merle is surprisingly forthright: "I don't believe at all that it's an immortal principle. I believe it can be perfectly destroyed. That's what happened to mine, which was a very good one to start with."[16]

Madame Merle and Gilbert Osmond have been lovers and Pansy is the issue of their union. In spite of her lack of free will,

Pansy provides a note of hope, for she embodies a major virtue of each "parent": Osmond's love of the beautiful and his flawless taste; Madame Merle's sense of the perfect; and Isabel's unflinching integrity. Pansy is the balance of cultivated taste and moral integrity. (These two ideals eventually fuse in Isabel Archer, but at greater cost and to greater effect, as she is the greater spirit.) Isabel was captivated by a cultivated man, one seemingly removed from the strife and struggle of the world as he walked up an Italian hillside in the sunlight. Not unnoticed, however, was the dainty girl he held by the hand. Isabel promises Pansy that she will return to Rome; we hope that, as a result, the child's individuality and identity will be salvaged.

Although, as Madame Merle predicted, Isabel rapidly became accustomed to her money, she still felt a certain discomfort about it, and sought an opportunity for generosity to one she considered supremely worthy: "I care very much for money, and that's why I wish Mr. Osmond to have a little."[17] Her wealth, which might have brought her freedom, made her vulnerable. As Henrietta prophesied, her fortune became "a curse in disguise." As it was a gift, Isabel felt beholden, morally obliged to use it generously. Freed of the external exigencies of the material, apparently unfettered by the tyranny of things, her obligation to choose aright was heightened.

In addition to satisfying her moral sensibilities, her money allowed her to indulge her obsession for pattern and story. To make sense out of her inheritance from her uncle, she must do something she could not have accomplished without it. Marriage to Gilbert Osmond fitted this scheme. As Ralph Touchett remarks, "Under the guise of caring only for intrinsic values, Osmond lived exclusively for the world."[18] "Alas, the real free spirits are not those who make a profession of it!"[19]

We are, in effect, given two "portraits," one of Isabel Archer and one of Isabel Osmond. "By presenting the events of the omitted years not directly, but retrospectively, James has been able to get the very telling effect of juxtaposing two similar, yet vastly different 'portraits of his lady.'"[20] Ralph finds that Isabel, "the free, keen girl had become quite another person; what he

saw was a fine lady who was supposed to represent something....She represented Gilbert Osmond."[21] Isabel, however,
never becomes merely a representative. She never completely
merges into her environment of artificial "Thursday evenings,"
much to her husband's disappointment. Her liberty has been
curtailed, her spontaneity and enthusiasm dampened, but her
protestant hatred of authority and her revulsion at the surrender
of will are never successfully suppressed.

Probably the most crucial moral meditation in *Portrait of a Lady*
is Isabel's interior monologue before the dying fire in Rome, as
she considers her motives for marrying Osmond and the reasons
her marriage failed:

> He had told her he loved the conventional; but there was a sense in
> which this seemed a noble declaration....She went with him freely,
> and his warning contained nothing ominous. But when, as the
> months elapsed, then she had seen where she really was....It was
> the house of darkness, the house of dumbness, the house of
> suffocation. Osmond's beautiful mind gave it neither light nor air;
> Osmond's beautiful mind indeed seemed to peep down from a
> small high window and mock at her. Under all his culture, his
> cleverness, his amenity, under his good nature, his facility, his
> knowledge of life, his egotism lay hidden like a serpent in a bank of
> flowers.[22]

While one of Osmond's reasons for marrying Isabel was no
doubt her wealth, he was probably quite sincere when he said,
"Money's a horrid thing to follow, but a charming thing to
meet."[23] He would not have married Henrietta were she "ten
times the heiress" that Isabel was. Certainly, too, the idea of
possessing Isabel as a beautiful object among his treasures
appealed to him, but this was not his sole consideration: "It has
made me better, loving you; it has made me wiser and easier and
— I won't pretend to deny — brighter and nicer and even
stronger....Upon my honour, I don't see why we shouldn't get
on."[24]

The mature Isabel, in her bleak and dry-eyed despair, considers
what led Osmond to hate her: "He had plenty of contempt, and it
was proper his wife should be as well-furnished; but that she

should turn the hot light of her disdain upon his own conception of things, this was a danger he had not allowed for."[25] Isabel is hated by one she has loved and trusted and to whom she had "so anxiously and yet ardently given herself";[26] moreover, she is hated for what she recognizes to be the best in herself, her free-enquiring mind and moral integrity. Isabel realizes that because "she had liked him so much" she "had pretended that there was less of her than there really was."[27]

When Isabel is called to the bedside of her beloved and dying cousin, it is only after great internal conflict that she decides to go. "Marriage meant that in such a case as this, when one had to choose, one chose as a matter of course for one's husband."[28] How many women still feel that they must "choose as a matter of course" in the same way Isabel does? She has matured, learning of the relationship between Serena Merle and her husband. The young girl who came to Gardencourt with an overwhelming desire to live has become a tired woman who returns to "envy Ralph his dying."

> Deep in her soul — deeper than any appetite for renunciation — was the sense that life would be her business for a long time to come. And at moments there was something inspiring, almost enlivening, in the conviction. It was proof of strength — it was proof she should some day be happy again.[29]

Ralph's dying words support her faith: "I don't believe that such a generous mistake as yours can hurt for more than a little."[30] If James does intend these fancies to be taken as serious predictions, Isabel will be freed by some force other than her own volition. Her reasons for returning and remaining in Rome support this position.

She returns to Pansy but she is also responsive to Osmond's appeal to preserve appearances.

> I've an ideal of what my wife should do and should not do. She should not travel across Europe alone, in defiance of my deepest desire, to sit at the bedside of other men. I'm not aware that we're divorced or separated; for me we're indissolubly united. You are nearer to me than any human creature, and I'm nearer to you. It may be a disagreeable proximity; it's one, at any rate, of our own

deliberate making...we should accept the consequences of our actions, and what I value most in life is the honour of the thing.[31]

Isabel reacts the only way she can: "His last words were not a command, they constituted a kind of appeal...He spoke in the name of something sacred and precious — the observance of a magnificent form."[32]

Isabel returns to Osmond out of fidelity to her ideal commitment to marriage. There are "certain obligations involved in the very fact of marriage...quite independent of the quality of enjoyment extracted from it."[33] Isabel is acutely aware that she is free to choose; and it is proof of her maturity that she never attempts to place the responsibility for her fate on other shoulders. "It seems to me I shall always be ashamed. One must accept one's deeds. I married him before all the world."[34]

Marriage and "the observance of a magnificent form" are, for Isabel, "transcendent and absolute." When Isabel, with great dignity, says to Madame Merle, "I think I should like never to see you again," she combines the moral strength that has always been hers with an appropriateness and refinement beyond even the polished and perfect, and evil, Madame Merle.

When we remember that at the novel's close Isabel is only twenty-eight, we may find her unswerving commitment entirely misplaced. Her fidelity to her step-daughter is admirable, but something a contemporary heroine would "try to work out in a new context." Readers today think that, to the extent that Isabel was the victim of conniving opportunism, she would be justified in leaving Osmond and should be free to do so without crippling guilt. Yet Isabel is too honest not to see the degree of her own responsibility and greatly affected by the sanctity of the promise given. Most contemporary readers would view Isabel's final decision as commitment to waste. Should we keep promises? Should we honour our vows? No matter what? Our society is full of ambivalence; Isabel Archer is a haunting incarnation of other standards, other assumptions, another manifestation of grace.

It is significant that James leaves the ending of Isabel's story ambiguous, with considerable hope that "she should some day be happy again"; happiness for Isabel, as we have seen, implies freedom in large measure. It is entirely possible that James was showing us the weight of social institutions upon women in order to show these institutions up. "James's fiction is centrally concerned with freedom, its concern is also with all that is seen to constrict freedom — with law, power and authority."[35] A century later, in a more open society, women struggle and push society's authority to its limits, but complete breaks, even for those who, unlike Isabel, have "marketable skills," are often virtually impossible. Women still return to husbands for whom they feel contempt because of the crushing weight of economic or social pressure.

ANNE OF GREEN GABLES
by
L.M. MONTGOMERY

This perennial favourite is increasingly popular through its stage and television versions. These renditions of the story are so well and favourably known that newer editions of the novel are likely to sport pictures from them.

The chronicle of Anne Shirley is the story of a female orphan. The novel is set in Prince Edward Island; although the island has no monopoly on sexist attitudes towards children, there is no question that male children are more useful, more cost-efficient and more welcome. Throughout the novel runs the theme of male achievement, and Anne, an intellectually curious little girl, is an anomaly. However, in spite of the strict division of labour between males and females, women on the island have a sense of worth and a knowledge that their domestic labour is essential to the functioning of that economic unit, the farm.

Anne is the "wrong" sex, but the reader is likely to be caught by her charm and will be pulling with her from the start. Matthew, a diffident bachelor farmer, finds his declining years brightened by the ebullient red-haired orphan. Marilla is the archetypal un-married sister-housekeeper-companion in her iron-willed no-nonsense approach to life and love. She is practical and pragmatic. Anne, with her imagination and dreams, is the archetypal child in every one of us. As she christens objects in the natural world with magical names, some of that magic rubs off on even the most jaded reader. As we respond to her schemes and pranks, we respond to the child in ourselves.

The school-teacher who can't teach is male in this story — a welcome change from the stereotype female of many tales. The teacher who nourishes the intellects and imaginations of the children in her care, we are happy to discover, is Miss Stacey. The enmity, rivalry and young love between Anne and Gilbert is moving, but it is difficult for a contemporary reader to accept that Anne "stays home with Marilla" and at the end of high school has "as much education as a girl can be comfortable with." That institutions of higher learning the world over should be entirely male preserves gave way only gradually and grudgingly to the idea that exceptional women, under unusual circumstances, could be admitted — if not taken too seriously. "Unusual circumstances" often meant a lack of sexual attractiveness. "What else can she do?" "Look at her — how will she ever catch a husband?" Higher education was often a sign of failure in a woman. The natural woman was supposed to want love and to cherish a man, a home and children. Moreover, she was not expected to want anything more. (These attitudes still linger in many communities.) Small wonder the missionary movement found so many adherents among intelligent, rural women! There were few other outlets for their imaginations once the marital gauntlet had been run. Anne, who is headstrong as well as bright, is tamed by the system. Her spunk is redirected from self-aggrandizement to service, which makes her an acceptable heroine for her time.

When we are impatient with Montgomery's story because of its blatant sexism, several things must be kept in mind. First, Montgomery went about as far as she could go with Anne and still have her beloved of the readers for whom she wrote. Anne the girl could take initiative, compete and succeed; to a certain extent she was more engaging for it. But female conformity, modesty and sacrifice were demanded of Anne the woman in the final chapters. It is tempting to speculate what would have happened had Matthew and Marilla adopted "Andrew" rather than "Anne." Andrew, had he won the scholarship, would have been off to Queen's with everyone's blessings and Marilla, it is certain, would have had to leave Green Gables. Perhaps one moral of the story is that it's a good thing, after all, to have a "girl around the house." A boy may go off to college.

It is important for readers of *Anne of Green Gables*, and indeed of all the Montgomery books, to see them in their own time and place. One of Anne's initial charms is that she is outspoken and headstrong — the orphan who will survive, imagination intact. Only when she is cherished does her gracious nature emerge. When she is embraced by the community, she is well content to adopt its central values. Anne the heroine is alive and well, asking soul-searching questions across the years as she responds to pressure not only with sacrifice but with imagination and energy, with hope and grace.

THE PROMISE
by
SOMERSET MAUGHAM

Somerset Maugham had a genius for creating a scene that illuminates an entire personality. It is for this reason, above all, that his short fiction translates so readily into film. In *The Promise*, the raconteur joins a friend who is eating a restaurant lunch alone. They seem to connect by chance. Lady Elizabeth Vermont, the hero and keeper of the promise, is a fifty-year-old woman whose "ravaged beauty made the fresh and blooming comeliness of youth a trifle insipid." "She became notorious for her profligacy."[36] She married and divorced regularly and in between had a succession of lovers she made no effort to keep secret:

> Her name stank in the nostrils of decent people. She was a gambler, a spendthrift, and a wanton. But though unfaithful to her lovers she was constant to her friends and there always remained a few who would never allow, whatever she did, that she was anything but a very nice woman. She had candour, high spirits and courage. She was never a hypocrite.... She was one of those blessed

persons who say quite fearlessly what they think (thus saving much useful time). She was always willing to talk (with a diverting humour) of her lurid past.[37]

Lady Elizabeth Vermont is not merely a character of "loose morals and a tender heart." She is, the narrator tells us, a "very nice woman, an honest woman, generous and sincere."

Maugham is inviting us to analyze morality in *The Promise*. Are sexual irregularities, excesses or many successive matings sufficient cause for one's name to stink "in the nostrils of decent people"? Obviously, part of the answer is yes. But what of the decent people? What is the basis for their judgement? Do they, in their decency, consider it "decent" behaviour to judge other people whom they know of but do not know? Are they too busy being self-righteous to be righteous?

Maugham asks these questions subtly in *The Promise*. (He asks them more directly in *The Judgement Seat*.) The motive behind the act may be all important. It may be honest and sincere to stay with one partner until death. It may also be dishonest and hypocritical not to change partners, or avoid partnership altogether. Maugham suggests that, unless bonds are those of love, no one should feel constrained. He seems also to suspect that those not honouring Eros may well be serving Thanatos.

Appearance and reality are at odds in *The Promise*. We seem to be asked to accept that "notwithstanding everything" Lady Elizabeth was an honest woman. When she was forty, she married a boy of twenty-one. Some of the "friends who had stuck with her through thick and thin" now deserted her for "the boy's sake." "The fact remains that she made him an admirable wife...his happiness seemed her only concern. No one could doubt that she loved him devotedly."[38]

After ten years of ideal marriage, however, Peter Vermont fell "madly in love" with a pleasant young girl, Barbara Canton, who was "pretty in a fair and fluffy way." Immediately after lunch, at the table where Peter had proposed to Barbara, Lady Elizabeth is to meet him to offer him a divorce. Robert Canton, Barbara's father, is described by Lady Elizabeth Vermont as "a stuffy old thing. I very much doubt if he'd let Barbara marry Peter if I divorced him. And for me, you know, it isn't of the smallest consequence: one divorce more or less."[39] It is before the day of no-fault divorce.

The reader learns that when Peter proposed to her, Lady Elizabeth promised that "when he wanted his release he should have it." It seemed to be expected that an older woman cannot indefinitely interest a younger man. (We are learning not to be racist in our loves, but ageist and sexist we remain. The idea of the older man and the younger woman is accepted, condoned, even advocated, yet the idea of the older woman with the younger man, meets with stubborn moralistic resistance.)

In *The Ambassadors*, Henry James examines the attraction between a young man and a middle-aged woman. In a poem called "Portrait of a Lady," T.S. Eliot presents the same phenomenon without any sense of taboo. It is certain, however, that in our society, older men become distinguished while older women become invisible.

Lady Elizabeth has made a promise: she will keep it in style. She knows well the difference between loving and possessing and has no desire to possess a man whose love is elsewhere. Leaving her luncheon companion,

> she held herself very erect and the poise of her head was gallant. She was a slim and lovely figure so the people looked at her as she passed. I saw her bow graciously to some acquaintance who raised his hat, and I thought that never in a thousand years would it occur to him that she had a breaking heart.[40]

Lady Elizabeth Vermont exhibits generosity and compassion by offering divorce to a man she passionately loves. Whatever we think of her moral position, which is certainly ambiguous, we admire her grace and courage.

TO THE LIGHTHOUSE
by
VIRGINIA WOOLF

Virginia Woolf is a key figure in feminist thought. By writing *To the Lighthouse* about Mrs. Ramsay, the beautiful nurturing hostess mother, and Mr. Ramsay, the abstract gloomy philosopher spiritually bound to the letter,she conjectured: "I did for myself what psychoanalysts do for their patients, I expressed some very long held and deeply felt emotion and in expressing it I explained it and then laid it to rest."[41]

Like all Virginia Woolf's work, *To the Lighthouse* can be studied from a variety of points of view. James Ramsay, a son, looks at the lighthouse and ponders: "So that was the Lighthouse, was it? No, the other was also the Lighthouse. For nothing was simply one thing. The other was the Lighthouse too."[42] *To The Lighthouse* is about many things, but it is certainly about the pressures to conform to what Grace Stewart has seen as the usual female roles of Persephone and Demeter. Stewart analyses Lily, who, as artist and appendage of the Ramsay menage, cannot be circumscribed by either role. Lily " stands outside mother, wife and even daughter roles, threatening her own identity by rejecting them, and trying instead to nourish via her art."[43] Mrs. Ramsay, the central figure and pivot of the novel, is seen in relation to Lily.

In some ways, Lily rivals Mrs. Ramsay as the main focus of interest for the reader. Some readers are more fascinated with Lily's response to Mrs. Ramsay and to her memories of Mrs. Ramsay than they are with what Prue, Mrs. Ramsay's biological daughter, calls "the thing itself." Mrs. Ramsay can relate to Lily only as independent and as yet unravished maiden, not to Lily as artist. Mrs. Ramsay scorns modern artists in general, cares "not a fig" for Lily's painting and insists that "an unmarried woman has missed the best in life." Mrs. Ramsay, as she sits for Lily, muses, "with her little Chinese eyes and her puckered-up face she would never marry; one could not take her painting very seriously."[44]

People of whatever sex or marital status may consider their state to be the "best in life." We claim as a society to accept with great equanimity a number of ways of living. But do we? How much real tolerance, let alone understanding, do we have for those with different life-styles? We have the right, of course, to applaud or bemoan our own choices, but do we have the right to insist, as Mrs. Ramsay does, that one style of life is "best"? Like most people, Mrs. Ramsay is a many-sided creature. She is the

> good mother who is reverenced, compassionate, charitable,
> beautiful and intuitive. She is also a terrible mother who is severe,
> vain, high handed, willful, commanding, stern, shortsighted,
> frightening, perhaps heartless in her own way. In both aspects she
> is irresistible.[45]

Mrs. Ramsay treats life as a work of art: as Lily observes, she "can
make of the moment something permanent" the way the artist
attempts to do.

> "That's my mother" thought Prue. Yes, Minta should look at her,
> Paul Rayley should look at her. That is the thing itself, she felt, as if
> there were only one person like that in the world; her mother. And,
> from having been quite grown up, a moment before, talking with
> the others, she became a child again.[46]

Mrs. Ramsay is the mother who holds her children, her guests and
her husband in the palm of her hand. Is she simply "giving, giving,
giving" as Lily once describes a woman's family life? Mrs. Ramsay
certainly gives a great deal — to husband, children and friends —
and her inclusion of everyone in her care and interest is moving. Is
there, however, another, less pleasant aspect to this beautiful,
nurturing woman? Does she manipulate as well as love and enjoy
those around her? As she match-makes with her guests, is there
perhaps a touch of the young Emma in this apparently mature
and fulfilled woman? After Mrs. Ramsay's death, Lily recalls: "So
they were sent for walks together...What was this mania of hers
for marriage?"[47] One thing is certain: Mrs. Ramsay has power and
her ability to attract is unchallenged. Although Mrs. Ramsay is
still present after her death, the last direct contact the reader has
with her is in one of her exhilarating moods of domestic triumph
in living. It is an intricately worked and intimate human exchange
carried on without speech:

> ...he was watching her. She knew what he was thinking. You are
> more beautiful than ever. And she felt very beautiful. Will you not
> tell me just for once that you love me?...But she could not do it; she
> could not say it. Then, knowing that he was watching her, instead
> of saying anything she turned, holding her stocking, and looked at
> him. And as she looked at him she began to smile, for though she

had not said a word, he knew, of course he knew, that she loved him. He could not deny it. And smiling she looked out of the window and said (thinking to herself, nothing on earth can equal this happiness), 'Yes you were right. It's going to be wet tomorrow.' She had not said it, but he knew it. And she looked at him smiling. For she had triumphed again.[48]

An aura of mystery somehow surrounds Mrs. Ramsay: she epitomizes the perfect wife-and-mother figure whose joy is apparently found in nurturing, guiding and controlling her husband, household and family. The flowers that she is forever growing, picking, carrying and arranging symbolize her grace in the midst of unrelenting responsibility and physical work. She is the centre and the fixed point in the turning world of everyone else. Mrs. Ramsay fills this role with grace and responds to its pressures with serenity. Everyone feeds from her bounty — physically, psychologically and emotionally. So committed is she to her role that she can imagine no other as satisfying for any woman: ultimately she may be "as one-sided and life-denying as her husband."[49] Obviously, Woolf means Mrs. Ramsay to be ambiguous — to make us think and rethink the roles of wife and mother, their power and their pitfalls.

Does Mrs. Ramsay believe, with the men of the story, that "Women can't paint, women can't write"? What effect do such convictions have on women's own work? Is the inadequacy of the work pre-ordained because women can't paint, can't write? Does the statement, carried in women's unconscious, affect the quality of their work?...Do they lessen their chances to produce great art by identifying positionally or sexually with breeders of children, sympathetic women who "can't write, can't paint"?[50] Not only are there no definitive answers to these questions, there are really no answers at all. But the novel asks the questions and it provides a starting point.

> Whereas Mrs. Ramsay, the female artist of human relations, receives reverence and love and whereas Mr. Carmichael, the male artist of poetry, receives accolades, the female artist in *To the Lighthouse* is labelled "a peevish, ill-tempered dried up old maid." While these words are Lily's own, she is expressing the view she is certain others have of her. There are other possibilities: *To The*

Lighthouse illustrates the destructive nature of a metaphysical belief in strong, immutably fixed gender identities — as represented by Mr. and Mrs. Ramsay — whereas Lily Briscoe (an artist) represents the subject who deconstructs this opposition, perceives its pernicious influence and tries as far as is possible in a still rigidly patriarchal order to live as her own woman, without the crippling definitions of sexual identity to which society would have her conform.[51]

As we read a story about a woman who *can* paint by a woman who *can* write, the position of the female artist and her interaction with her society haunt us. We remember Lily's single moment of exaltation, which has parallels with Mrs. Ramsay's "married" epiphany. Lily considers her painting and her life in concert: "She had only escaped by the skin of her teeth....She had been looking at the tablecloth, and it had flashed upon her that she would move the tree to the middle, and need never marry anybody, and she felt an enormous exaltation."[52] Lily, too, experiences grace and a moment of glory.

The stereotyping of women has probably altered since 1927, when *To The Lighthouse* was first published. (The book is still immensely popular.) In this regard it may be important to ask ourselves if we are outgrowing the stereotypes it portrays. Do we take seriously artists who are female? Do we have high regard for women and men who concentrate upon the arts of living and nurturing? In short, do we embrace freedom of choice and accord each other respect for our life choices?

A TREASURE FOR TONY
by
LYN COOK

Tony is another young heroine who, instead of rebelling, tries to work, with grace, to change what she dislikes or fears in her life. Tony is a happy child in a loving home, a rarity in contemporary fiction. Still, Tony and her family are very much alive and therefore are not without problems. *A Treasure for Tony* is about problems and attempting to solve them, but it is not strictly a "problem" novel. While her problems may seem slight, any reader, remembering childhood, will recall the magnitude of its hurdles and changes. Tony — Antonia — has an idyllic home on a farm that has mysteries, hidden treasures, secret ladies — all the things that can nourish a young girl's vivid imagination. Old Ned, an ancient man full of goodwill and good yarns, came with the farm, and the affection that develops between him and Tony is sensitively depicted. It is the sort that often springs up between the old and the young, an understanding that the overworked, overwrought, responsible middle generation cannot share.

During the story, urban sprawl threatens to overtake the farm; the new life and energy that immigrants bring to a region and country touch and enhance Tony and her family; racial tensions, marital breakup, the thrill of adopting a child — all these timeless and contemporary "issues" are the very fabric of Tony's life. A young girl's first experience of the death of someone near and dear is treated with a refreshing naturalness, without the self-consciousness that seems to surround death and dying in much contemporary fiction. Tony learns, too, that we never really own the land on which we live — even if it is the land from which we make our living. Economic pressures can always force one to "give up" one's home and, often, with it an important part of one's personal identity. The threat of banishment from the farm, however, is treated with great resourcefulness by our young heroine, who engages in a series of activities and adventures in her efforts to ward off the evil day. Sleigh rides do not become big business but they do make money and new friends. There is always the haunting hope, too, that "Good Adam's treasure" will be found, and that, with it, security will be assured.

Tony is a secret dancer who confides to a secret lady. She loves mystery and magic, and her faith in them is entirely justified. Such is the nature of enchantment, however, that it comes to Tony in unexpected ways. Joanna, Tony's friend, has her own secrets and her own problems. Together they learn, ride horses, misunderstand, hurt and heal each other. When Joanna says, "You're a funny kid with all your secrets. But never mind, you'll grow up soon enough," Tony keeps her own counsel, in spite of her irritation.

Tony's face grew hot at the remark. "You're a funny kid with all your secrets." But Joanna was wrong. She would always have secrets and dream her special dreams in the loft.[53]

Tony repeatedly acts with grace as she tries not to inflict her worry and hurt on others; while she does not always succeed, she makes an effort towards kindness and consideration in all her dealings. She is generous to other people and compassionate to animals.

The historical aspects of the novel are important. Clues and hints and guesses have to be followed to mysteries of the past: sunsets are needed to illuminate long-hidden messages. Grace casts out the arrogance of exaggerated self-importance. There is always respect as well as awe for "Good Adam" and for the past. A sense of responsibility to those who "went before" and to those who will "come after" prevails, for, left to our own devices, we are transients on this planet.

Tony strives to include everyone in her caring regardless of age (Old Ned and the young children stranded by snow), race (Katrine, Joanna) or origin (Gavin). This inclusion reaches back and forward in time, giving what has been called a "quiet novel" a resonance that will have staying-power in our imagination. Life has a fine way of "weaving tapestries." Knowing his story of long ago, Tony felt connected to Good Adam who once loved and cared for the farm: "Good Adam knows we're sorry to go, but at least we've celebrated the life of the farm in the best way we knew how."[54] Celebration, not ownership, is our proper business.

For the complex Isabel or for the good-hearted Tony, confrontation is likely to be with oneself rather than head-on with others. It is not an easy moral stance. It takes practice, self-knowledge and courage, particularly in times like ours, which stress a particular and sometimes narrow brand of assertiveness. Abstaining from pressure on others when you yourself are pressured is no mean accomplishment.

A Treasure for Tony presents ordinary people trying to deal with personal, domestic, vocational, economic and social problems — many of which are timeless and some of which are peculiar to our time. They are under many pressures: they respond to them with grace.

▲

CHAPTER FIVE

REBELLION UNDER PRESSURE

Get the thing done and let them howl.

NELLIE MCCLUNG'S CRY OF REBELLION is rousing. It encourages females to believe in their power to do things, to accomplish in arenas traditionally reserved for or controlled by males. It captures the conflict between the need for personal achievement and societal expectations of service to others.

Rebellion is a contemporary female response to narrowly defined sex roles and to the limitations imposed by marriage, the market-place, the professions and the arts upon all of us who are female, and considered secondary. The hatred of the female runs deep in our unconscious. The memories of societal pressures and the penalties extracted from those who will not comply make us both fear and crave rebellion. Rebellion takes guts, and those who have clothed and hidden their vulnerability may find it too risky. In this chapter we look at females who dare, and dare again.

Morag Gunn of Margaret Laurence's *The Diviners* tackles life and gains the courage to know and be — herself. She needs her strong will to rebel, in the short term at least, against the conventions of home, of school and the codes of behaviour prescribed for girls and women in almost every sphere. Morag's rebellion is often clumsy, and she suffers humiliations and defeats, but her surrender to any system is never complete. The novel takes us from Morag the orphaned child, who must take parents where she finds them, to Morag the mother, whose daughter is leaving home. Rebellion takes many forms — for example, the codes of the town must be seen and shed. At the same time the novel asks if anyone's rebellion against the pressures of her own Manawaka can ever be complete.

Like any analytical woman who wishes to have some control over her own life, Morag does a sabre dance with conventional morality, but she sometimes modulates to an accommodating foxtrot. Her marriage and the conformity and shrinking it requires constitute such a step, and we pity Morag as she tries to go on dancing long after the music fades. After her phoney and real selves collide, as they can only in Manawaka, her rebellions take a different turn. They become more creative, literally and figuratively. No longer empty, they empower her to move on in her development and bring her, still an outsider but transformed, a peculiar peace.

The Minerva Program is a contemporary tale of human effort, disappointment and vindication as old as the species. Minerva, the teen-aged centre of the fuss, rebels in the usual ways: against family values, against values of former friends. The pivotal rebellion in the novel, however, is against unjust accusation, and she uses everything in her power and that of her brother and friends to make justice prevail. Some minor rebellions are necessary en route, and the reader pulls with her and hails her well-deserved triumph.

Hansel and Gretel, in whatever version, portrays one of the most resourceful girls in fairy and folk tales. Gretel's rebellion takes a number of forms — deceit certainly, murder most joyous and theft galore. She is enterprising in her rebellion: the direct approach is not recommended when dealing with wicked witches. However, most impressive is Gretel's creative problem-solving. She suggests Hansel put forward sticks or chicken bones rather than his own finger, and that the witch herself — head first, if you please — test the temperature of the oven. It is she who unlocks Hansel's cage so that, the witch's loot in hand, they may return home together. Had Hansel been alone, the story would have ended abruptly and the witch eaten very well indeed. Gretel rebels under pressure to good effect.

It is easy to see Jo March of *Little Women* as the tomboy who eventually opts for petticoats and orderly marriage. But to do so is to underestimate the extent of her rebellion. She rebels against proper clothes and proper language and the opinion of what Emily Dickinson has called the "admiring bog." She rebels against the marriage market that even her semi-saintly mother accepts. She rebels against loveless marriage to a friend because she hankers for something more. Her rebellion is sometimes silly, sometimes courageous, but always real. It is no accident that, as the years pass, Amy and Meg blur, and Beth becomes a disembodied spirit, but Jo lives on in the imaginations of the many women whom she persuaded, as girls, to do it their own way.

Gone with the Wind, a civil-war story set in the South, has a heroine who suffers from being read superficially. She is frequently considered an egocentric conniving bitch; but, in fact, she is infinitely more complex than this one-dimensional description suggests. Scarlett O'Hara's stock-in-trade is rebellion, and, for her time and place, she is a remarkable rebel. Scarlett insists on running her own show; she refuses to think about war, but can do battle whenever she has to. She rebels by loving someone else's husband, by using her sexual powers to get what she wants and needs, by walking in the street pregnant, by running a business. She tackles work that is "beyond" women of her pampered background, and she rebels under the pressure each successive disaster life or her own nature foist upon her. Scarlett's story does not end with the bells or knells of conventional novels: it doesn't even end on the last page. Her form of procrastination —thinking about a new difficulty tomorrow so she can cope with the exigencies of today — has served her well, and, in the reader's continued story-making, will continue to do so.

All these women rebel against the situations they are in. While rebellion is never its own moral justification, and while its motives and forms are ever in need of scrutiny, the women have all been mightily provoked. Patriarchy usually rewards rebellious males and docile females; but the characters in this section challenge the clichés of societal expectations: they work, they struggle, they suffer, they act, they lay claim on life.

THE DIVINERS
by
MARGARET LAURENCE

In *The Diviners*, "the common female impulse to struggle free from social and literary confinements through strategic redefinitions of self, art and society"[1] is rendered incarnate in the writer, Morag Gunn. While there is a sense in which all women in life and fiction rebel silently and secretly or, in Emily Dickinson's words, "out loud" and openly, spunky Morag rebels in both ways. In *The Diviners*, Laurence examines the form, function and content of morality and finds that they often run counter to those of manners and social convention. Ultimately, Morag rejects empty forms and comes to terms with the thing itself. For example, Morag has little use for the Judeo-Christian God: "God knows what you are thinking. He knows, all right, all right. But is mean. Doesn't care. Or understand."[2] Yet Morag, another in the long line of orphaned female children whose powerful imaginations help to compensate for their loss, talks in her head to God. "Telling him that it was all His fault and this is why she is mad at Him. Because He is no good, is why."[3] To shake one's fist at the heavens, to blame whatever gods there be for our turmoil and suffering is, of course, a time-honoured custom. It is not, however, particularly common among fictional female children, and it distinguishes Morag as a robust and independent thinker at the outset. How unlike, for example, the dialogues the March sisters have with the Almighty!

Morag not only renounces God as an ever-ready help in trouble, she also gives humankind short shrift. She says, "That will be the day, when I try to please a living soul."[4] Such apparent lack of concern for others hardly qualifies Morag as a heroine of high moral stature, but it does indicate considerable strength. Upper-crust matrons in Manawaka may hurt her and even temporarily maim her, but she refuses to play victim to their bully.

In terms of manners, Morag could scarcely be more different from Jane Austen's Emma Woodhouse and Henry James's Isabel

Archer. Emma is the virtual centre of her charmed social circle; Morag is at the periphery of her far-from-charming one. At the outset, however, Morag is socially controlled even more than Emma. Emma is wealthy, educated, decked in sartorial splendour with surface manners beyond reproach. Morag, the changeling, is different from her peers in dress, hair-style, family and culture. Her language and social rituals separate her from the mainstream, as the finger code exemplifies. Emma is decidedly clever; Isabel's remarkable mind is much in evidence; but Morag describes herself as born bloody-minded. The most powerful image of the novel, Dan's painting of Morag, which he calls "Morag Dhu," reveals "her eyes, clearly and unmistakably the eyes of Morag, angry and frightened, frighteningly strong."[5] While her eyes are the focus of the portrait, her mind might accurately be described in similar terms.

Morag's inner strength combines with her social position to determine, in large measure, her reaction to school. She is no gentle Morag, meek and mild, sweetly obeying the system. Rather she learns self-defence and survival from the very first day. "She still does not know how to read. Some school this turned out to be. But has learned one thing for sure. Hang onto your shit and never let them know you are ascared."[6]

Just how essential Morag's bloody-mindedness is to her survival and development we learn through the contrasting story of Eva Winkler, her classmate. As with all fictional Eves before her, from the one in *Genesis* to Sylvia Fraser's in *The Candy Factory*, sex rules her way. Eva, like Morag, and for the same reasons, is on the outer edges of the social circle. She is obedient but, as Morag remarks, "gutless as a cleaned whitefish." Throughout the novel, Eva serves not only as a foil, but as a constant reminder of what Morag might have been. They begin school under the same trying conditions, but Eva succeeds in controlling neither her fear nor her bowels. Her inability to cope with school drastically reduces her chances of ever leaving Manawaka. Eva becomes pregnant, as Morag might well have done, and aborts herself. Not only does she remain in Manawaka; she assumes the role that would normally have fallen to Morag: caring for Christie and Prin and, eventually, for their graves. The inevitability of much of Eva's experience forces the reader to question a system that so conditions, controls and limits human life. We are also confronted with the double-edged sword of selflessness, always ranked high as a feminine virtue. Is self-sacrifice the sacrifice of the self? What does a high moral code demand of us, anyway? Are the demands significantly different for women and men?

The stereotype of the harsh, nagging, even cruel and generally unappealing female school teacher is unfortunately perpetuated by Morag's teacher, with her "butcherknife voice." The education of Morag's fertile imagination is really carried out by Christie Logan, a strangely displaced Christ figure. Christie, the garbage collecter and keeper of "the Nuisance Grounds," has pride in his "kin and clan" and a way with words. "By their garbage shall ye know them" is certainly one way to view the Connors and McVities of any community. This teller of tales, well aware of Morag's rebelliousness and sensitivity, teaches her about the deep social cleavages and class-consciousness of Hill Street. It is from him, too, that she learns of the legendary Piper Gunn, who led the Scottish exiles out of bondage to the promised land of Canada. Christie nourishes Morag's love of story and language:

> Morag is working on another story as well. In another scribbler. She does not know where it will come from. It comes into your head, and when you write it down, it surprises you, because you never knew what was going to happen until you put it down.[7]

Here we find Morag, whose religious attitudes are anything but conventional, becoming attracted to Jesus:

> Morag loves Jesus. And how. He is friendly and not stuck-up, is why. She does not love God. God is the one who decides which people got to die and when. Mrs. McKee in Sunday School says God is *LOVE* but this is baloney. He is mean and gets mad at people for no reason at all, and Morag wouldn't trust him as far as she can spit.[8]

Morag's moral sense shines through clearly: it is wrong to be remote and stuck up and to treat others according to whim rather than reason; it is right to be friendly. Here Morag's view of the conventionally male members of the divine family is similar to Rudy Wiebe's: in the Mennonite community in which he was raised, all the children knew that while God spoke High German, Jesus spoke Low German just as they did.

One of the most intriguing and difficult aspects of *The Diviners* is that it includes several different strains of fiction. One of these might, somewhat simplistically, be called the "adolescent-problem novel," although it is seldom the good fortune of this strain to be written with such fine, deft strokes. In fact, *The Diviners* contains three problem stories, of children unlike their peers facing prejudice, rejection and a "broken home." Morag, Jules and, eventually, Pique must confront these problems. The reasons for their alienation differ but in the eyes of a judgemental community appear to have the same roots. As self-righteous Mrs. Tate says, "The home, the home, always look to the home."

All three children adopt similar methods of coping with rejection. They cultivate a tough exo-skeleton, an inner strength and a dependence upon story. Morag and Jules have been drawn together since their days in elementary school. They share a view of society from what they consider to be a higher vantage point, which reveals very sharply the vile morals of the social and educational systems that reject them. Instead of revering institutions, Morag and Jules adopt heroes. These heroes, Piper Gunn and Rider Tonnerre, provide the stories upon which Morag's and Jules' strength and selfhood are to depend. At the outset, both loftily reject the society that will not let them participate in it. But the nature and duration of their rejection is a major difference between them. Jules rejects society permanently and loathes the audience from whom he earns his living. Morag rejects society, but on a temporary, conditional basis, exemplified by her attitude towards the journal *Veritas*: "They both despise *Veritas* now, and will continue to do so until something of theirs is printed therein."[9] Jules recognizes Morag's longing to achieve success in the world — "You want it so bad I can just about smell it on you"[10] — and shrewdly predicts what form Morag's success is likely to take.

The alienated-adolescent story in *The Diviners* is superseded by the traditional romance. After she has come to know Jules, sexually and otherwise, Jules goes to war and Morag goes to college. She is published in a small way, falls in love and marries a professor, in accordance with Jules' prophecy. Like the adolescent-problem novel, however, the romantic love story is outgrown: the wedding is not an ending, but a turning point. The feminist question, "Is there life after marriage?" is answered with a resounding "yes" if the heroine of romance deserts the hero. Morag describes her marriage as "living each other's fantasy somehow." Morag, the bloody-minded, has become Brooke's "little one." Brooke is delighted when Morag claims to have no past. Yet, like all grown women, she does have a past, and it regularly impinges upon her present. Brooke must suppress it whenever it threatens to surface and destroy the fantasy. Apparently Brooke would prefer Morag to remain static, not only with no past but also with no real future. As so often happens in life and in fiction, the female protagonist is forbidden to grow as an individual or as an artist after marriage. Unlike many novelists, however, Laurence does not abandon her heroine: for a spell only must she play Rapunzel trapped in the tower. "Maybe tower would be a better word for the apartment .... A lonely tower .... Rapunzel, Rapunzel, let down your long hair. Your long, straight, black hair ..."[11]

Brooke creates an image of an ideal wife and Morag struggles to conform to it. For a time, Morag represses the black Celt in her. She makes feeble attempts to avoid total submission — refusing, for example, to go to the hairdresser, in spite of Brooke's urging and arguing — but, for the most part, she succumbs, and in so doing must lie.

> Morag thinks of her smile. The eager agreement to go out. How many times has she lied to him before, or is this the first time? No, it is not the first time. She never thought of it that way before. It never seemed like lying. Now it does.[12]

For Brooke, fantasy is truth. Morag's small-town origins and apparent shyness convince him not only of her virginity, but of her innocence. In their first sexual encounter Brooke assumes that she has never seen a man naked and erect. Morag becomes increasingly aware of the gap between Brooke's ideal and her own reality, between her appearance, which conforms to his ideal, and her self, which cannot and will not. When Morag returns to Manawaka for Prin's funeral, her real and phony selves collide: "At this moment she hates it all, this external self who is at such variance with whatever or whoever remains inside the glossy painted shell. If anything remains, her remains."[13] At Prin's funeral Morag cries out not to Piper Gunn but to the God she had found remote and unfair. "Help me, God; I'm frightened of myself."[14] Morag may indeed be frightened of herself — the self she must confront in Manawaka — but once that fear has been named, the days of the glossy painted shell of appearance are numbered. Whether or not a divinity intervenes, this cry marks a turning-point.

Morag's rebellion, following fast upon Prin's funeral, is in some sense a return to the past. In an argument with Brooke, Morag uses Christie's language, her mother tongue, so to speak. Brooke, recognizing the connection between her past and her rebellion, begs her to forget the past, but this time she cannot. Instead she embraces it: Jules rescues her from the tower and refers to himself as the shaman in the ritual of her rebellion. Morag's will to survive reasserts itself in a kind of death and resurrection: a new life, Pique, is born. (Morag joins the host of female heroines who have one female child. To Hester's Pearl and Isabel's Pansy, Morag's Pique can be added.)

Whether there was any justification for Brooke's attempting a god-like creation of another human being, the fact of his pain, his rejection, must be faced. It is real and has grave moral implications. Yet, for Morag to be born or reborn, the old fantasy with Brooke must be discarded, at whatever cost. As she flies to Vancouver the rites of renunciation and initiation blur again.

It would be risky to underestimate the seductive appeal of the "little-one" syndrome, particularly for a woman who has suffered deprivation and hardship during her formative years. Independence is hard won and often cold comfort; many women understandably prefer bondage with ease to strenuous liberty.

The circumscribed life, the life of Austen's heroines, for example, offered certain freedoms that a contemporary woman with a story of her own dreams not of. She often, as Morag discovers, is too weary to dream. Interestingly enough, it is no longer the male hero, Piper Gunn, whose story sustains Morag. No more does his poetry, full of adventure and romance, uplift and encourage. Instead it is the straightforward prose of Catherine Parr Traill's *The Canadian Settlers Guide* of 1855 that becomes her touchstone. "In cases of emergency, it is folly to fold one's hands and sit down to bewail in abject terror. It is better to be up and doing."[15]

The most obvious and perhaps the central moral dilemma of *The Diviners* concerns the conception of Pique. The sterility of Morag's marriage to Brooke was of his choosing. When Morag realizes that she no longer wishes to bear his child, she has a primitive understanding that this means the marriage is over. Nevertheless, even the most liberal or lax of moral systems would hardly consider this a reason to conceive Jules' child in such haste:

> Would she have gone back if she hadn't been pregnant? At this moment she feels she would have. Was it only for that reason, after all, she had wanted to get pregnant so her leaving of Brooke would be irrevocable? So she would not be able to change her mind? And had chosen Jules so there wouldn't be the slightest chance of pretending the child was Brooke's. How many people had she betrayed? Had she even betrayed the child itself? This thought paralyses her.[16]

In *Feminist Criticism in the Wilderness*, Elaine Showalter argues that Margaret Atwood's novel *Surfacing* is "romantically asserting that women are closer to nature, to the environment, to a matriarchal principle at once biological and ecological."[17] When *Surfacing* is seen in the context of Atwood's work to date, and *The Diviners* in terms of Laurence's canon, there is some evidence that the back-to-nature motif in these works may be both feminist and typically Canadian. Unlike many of their fictional sisters of times past, the heroines of these texts become pregnant not so much by accident as by design.

Pique eventually accuses Morag of having conceived her

selfishly without considering Jules or Pique. Was Pique's conception irresponsible? If so, was it immoral? What moral base is flaunted or affirmed? "The awful daring of a moment's surrender which an age of prudence cannot retract. By this and this only have we existed."[18]

Morag does not ask Jules directly if he desires a child. She asks him rather if he would mind if she declined to try not to conceive. Jules's responsibility is reduced to a minimum. Yet he agrees to the awful daring and cannot reject the reality of his daughter and his fatherhood. Morag applies the same standard to Dan McRaith's fatherhood. She thinks of Dan's many children as Bridie's "choice, her hold on him. His choice as well. He had not said no to them."[19]

▲

It becomes clear that, whatever responsible parenthood may be, it involves a great deal more than not saying "no." Morag's motherhood and Jules's fatherhood are not settled for all time; they must be affirmed again and again as the bond between Morag and Pique is affirmed and apparently dissolved, only to be reaffirmed more strongly. Jules declares his fatherhood on his first visit: "She's yours, all right. But she's mine too, eh?"[20] Eventually Jules will give Pique his songs and his knife, his only memento from his own father.

The moral centre of *The Diviners* is the family. The consciousness of Dan's family prevents Morag from continuing her liaison with him. Morag's terrifying experience with Chas, with its accompanying fear of pregnancy, teaches her two moral lessons concerning self and family. She realizes that she, like mothers from the dawn of time, would kill to save her child. She also recognizes that she cannot risk sex with a man such as Chas for fear of conceiving his child. Morag is quite clear about this latter moral lesson, however, declaring it "not morality. Just practicality of spirit and flesh."[21] She strenuously resists the internal division of body and spirit that she experienced in her marriage to Brooke. Sexual manners in *The Diviners* may be askew, but sexual morality is unflinchingly based in responsibility to oneself and to one's descendants.

The emphasis on family — as Pique's birth and the fierce loyalty of Lazarus to his children indicate — is conventional, but the concept of family is not. Herein lies much of the book's strength and fascination, and also the paradox that causes the hysteria of frightened and superficial readers. *The Diviners*, a deeply religious book, has itself been put under pressure by public censure of isolated content. As Marshall McLuhan warned us some time ago, "fragmentation is the only obscenity," and the rejection of *The Diviners*, which seems to have been based upon isolated fragments, is the only obscenity involved. Banning this noble text tells of a community's fear and ignorance of language and literature, perhaps of life itself. It may also hark back to the specific distrust of the woman novelist evident from at least the time of Elizabeth Gaskell and the furor over her novel *Ruth*.*

The sense of being related to one another is stressed throughout *The Diviners*. The ties that bind include blood, of course, but there are more inclusive ties as well, those of the inheritors. Royland's heir is A-Okay, not by blood but in the sharing of a gift. Morag is an inheritor not only of Piper Gunn but also of Christie: "Christie, I used to fight a lot with you, Christie, but you've been my father to me." Christie's response is telling and succinct. "Well, I'm blessed."[22] Morag is also, in a curious and often amusing way, the heir of Catherine Parr Traill, as woman writer and perhaps, metaphorically, as pioneer. She is, in all aspects, someone's heir.

This concept of continuity, whether we will or not, is one upon which *The Diviners* insists and one upon which human dignity rests. Pique is, of course, Morag's inheritor, but so too are younger writers and Laurence's readers. The intense sense of family depicted in *The Diviners* is not founded upon the traditional family structure. It reassures us, however, that whatever forms

---

*Note: Both Gaskell in *Ruth* (1853) and Laurence in *The Diviners* (1974) have moved the centre of their stories from the heterosexual couple to focus on the connections between parent and child.

ebb and flow, our need for one another, for continuity and commitment remain.

Morag has a story of her own, albeit one complicated by stories and about stories. There is no important question such as "Who will she marry?" There is not even a series of questions. Rather, *The Diviners* is a continuous questioning of society and ourselves. Finally, as surely as John Fowles' *The French Lieutenant's Woman*, the book is a questioning of fiction itself.

While the structure of the novel is contained within the memory and experience of Morag, she cannot tell what is memory and what is the shaping and embellishment we humans, because we are natural myth makers, give to our memories. The subjective nature of experience demands that all ethics be, in a sense, situational ethics, for even with good will and imagination we have difficulty encompassing multiple points of view. Morag at least understands our isolation and the impossibility of the communication for which we all long:

> Whatever is happening to Pique is not what I think is happening, whatever that may be. What happened to me wasn't what anyone else thought was happening and maybe not even what I thought was happening at the time .... What really happened? A meaningless question. But one I keep trying to answer, knowing there is no answer.[23]

The Diviners is a many-storied thing and each reader, with each reading, will experience a somewhat different text.

Morag creates a legend based on Christie that is and is not the man; her novels are and are not herself. Who has been real and who imagined? All have been both, it seems. Morag accepts and occasionally even enjoys a truth distilled from not one but many stories. There is no true version of any story, even the story of an historical event such as the Riel rebellion. Pique and A-Okay are still young enough to want definite answers. What they will eventually find, as Pique is beginning to do, is that truth is found not by clearing away stories, but by gathering and continuing them. Pique, it is certain, will write the song that Jules never wrote for himself. Although Morag has more self-determination than most female heroes dare to dream of, the end of her story is in its beginning. She is back on the social periphery, considered eccentric. Yet her need to be aloof from society is no longer motivated by ignorance. Guided by her "practicality of spirit and body," she cannot follow the dictates of social conformity for fear that her inner consistency, attained at great cost, be threatened. Morag's struggle, lost almost entirely, it seemed, during her marriage to Brooke, is to be what she seems. The centre she occupies is surrounded by a web of interrelatedness woven of her own experience, her ancestors, her inheritors. She is also at the point at which the real and the imagined intersect and become indistinguishable.

> Pique is departing for Galloping Mountain:
> So long. Go with God, Pique.
> Ma, you have some pretty funny expressions.
> Now then, don't I just? [24]

Christie has been blessed at his departure. Now Pique is blessed upon her way. So, *The Diviners* seems to suggest, are we all, all blessed.

THE MINERVA PROGRAM
by
CLAIRE MACKAY

> "I didn't do it. I didn't do it!" She turned and ran from the office. [25]

An unjust accusation and conviction, particularly when it deprives you of your favourite pursuit and inflicts multiple doses of an activity you detest, is enough to make the most serene and pliable of natures rebel. Add to these injustices, disappointment in you or the lack of respect for you engendered by authority figures, and only one question remains: how will you respond? Some women respond with despondency, some with undirected anger and bitterness. Others rebel. This rebellion can be destructive or restorative.

Minerva, after humiliation and frustration, decides upon a creative, if somewhat desperate and risky plan. For the execution of this plan she solicits the help of her peers (her younger brother, James, actually volunteers) rather than that of powerful adult figures. Adults are affected by her resolve, but not part of the decision making, planning or enactment. Like Gretel and Hansel, the young people in *The Minerva Program* learn to depend upon one another. As they proceed, they also grow more caring and more sophisticated in their attitudes and dealings with parents and teachers.

In *The Minerva Program*, Claire Mackay neatly challenges a number of stereotypes while stopping short of ruining her tale with good intentions. The heroine is extra tall, skinny and computer-friendly; her male friends are a short Portuguese boy and her younger brother. Her mother, Victoria, is a whiz in mathematics and works outside her home, as does her father; but her father takes cooking lessons, plans to work in a restaurant and does the cooking at home. The heroine is Jamaican-Canadian and her best friend Sophie is Greek-Canadian and a Dickens freak.

Another friend is a bright and decent man-crazy punk: "Minerva chuckled and glanced again at Barbara Fairfax. Wild make-up. Crazy pink hair. And that one huge earring, big as a saucer. But a good face underneath it all, with a mouth ready to laugh and thoughtful blue eyes. Minerva was suddenly sure that the punk stuff was just a disguise, something for the real Barbara to hide behind."[26] All in all, the idea that appearance masks reality is a cornerstone of life and literature. Mackay, while making this insight pretty obvious, keeps it subservient to the story-line and allows the reader to take morality in through her pores rather than be brow-beaten.

Minerva, the modern-day goddess of wisdom, undergoes such contemporary traumas as displacement from city core to suburban wasteland and the empowering elitism offered by high-tech. It is to our wise heroine's credit that she finds and creates life in suburbia and grows beyond the heady superiority that successfully, and sometimes permanently, seduces: "The future seemed a land without limits, and she felt again that surge of joy as she realized she would be one of those who explored that land, who commanded the future. And she would leave Sophie and her mother and all the rest who were stuck in the past, without regret, without a backward look"[27]

Minerva discovers that mothers cannot be left behind with impunity; willy-nilly they're on the trip with us. She learns instead that relationships shift, teeter precariously and grow. Part of the shift occurs when the daughter has a chance to be mother to the woman. When Victoria feels impotent and discouraged by the computer takeover, Minerva teaches her how she and her co-workers, human beings, can beat technology at its own game. Feelings for fathers change, too. Fathers repair things when we are children. As we mature we begin to count on ourselves and our peers. In addition, Minerva learns that ponderous nineteenth-century fiction can be relevant to late-twentieth-century problem solving. How much richer friendship is when people have different major passions! Friendship may be laughing at the same jokes, loyalty, intimacy and the celebration and respect for difference. Even kid brothers, those ever-present liabilities of life, can be, on occasion, assets — not entirely an unmixed curse, after all. "She looked at the three of them. Sophie. Angelo. James. They were her friends. Her true and loyal friends. How could she ever have thought she didn't need them?" [28]

The importance of social codes is stressed in *The Minerva Program*. There is a way to talk and a way to behave in your peer group, which you violate at your peril. The moral implications of the book, however, are extensive and surprisingly complex. The unvarnished truth, for example, is sometimes out of the question.

> ..."Soph, can you get out after supper?" Sophie's dad was really strict about her going out at night. "Not if I tell the truth. Can't you just hear it? 'Dad, I have to go out for a while to break into the school. Is that okay?' So I'll say I'm going to the library."[29]

Extreme measures are often required to remedy extreme injustices, and the causes of justice and truth seem, to protagonists and readers, well worth the deception of break and enter.

Cooperation and team-work prevail. The principle of fidelity to the inner group and the needs of its members is upheld. "James was quiet for a few seconds, then he took his sister's hand and said 'You in trouble, Min? . . . Then I'll help! I'll climb up and go through the window.'" [30]

Psychological abuse by teachers of young people is much publicized. Less often remarked is teacher abuse by adolescents. Mackay makes all the adults in this young-adult story not only entirely believable, but multi-dimensional as well. The male principal is simply a laughable caricature, but the female teacher is redeemed. The detested and misunderstood "Pickle" emerges as Hildegarde Dill, a human being, not a monster, and a telling symbol of Minerva's advance toward maturity.

Mackay uses interior monologue to great effect. Minerva has a wonderfully ironic sense of humour. Her wry comments add immeasurably to the enjoyment and progression of the story.

> And so, folks, she announced silently, we come to the end of an average day in the life of Minerva Wright. A race riot in the lobby, a fight with her best friend, a disaster in gym, and a mad killer loose in the plaza....Tune in tomorrow for more exciting adventures. [31]

This comic detachment — the ability to stand just a little outside one's situation — is fundamental to the ethical life. Minerva proves herself not only the teen-age goddess of wisdom, but of justice, hope and reconciliation. In many senses, an ideal hero for our time.

HANSEL AND GRETEL

Recent studies in semiotics have shown us that the position of words influences their potency. This story is about Gretel — and Hansel! She is the prime mover and the primary focus of attention. (Snow White, after all, is more important than the dwarves, and the princess more interesting than the pea.) However, Hansel is usually pictured as older and as male, so it is not surprising that his name comes first: the position of privilege. Gretel, younger and female though she is, is the more imaginative and active child, just as surely as Lucy, young and female, is the prime mover in *The Lion, the Witch and the Wardrobe*. They both rebel when given life-and-death-pressures. They are both frightened, but they fight back.

There are many versions of *Hansel and Gretel*. An early written example is *The Babes in the Wood,* in which the "pretty babes" die of weariness, hunger and exposure. It remains only for the birds to cover them gently with leaves. In some of the early versions there is a sense of fate being in control, and the babes are not only pretty but helpless and hapless. The figure of the step-mother is another variable. She appears in about half the renderings of this story, and she is exceedingly important. When the going gets rough, she resents having to feed and keep another woman's children. In many dramatic productions of the story, the roles of the step-mother and witch are played by the same actor, and children are encouraged to make the connection. According to Bruno Bettelheim, evil step-mothers are not placed in tales and subsequently much maligned, to make life more difficult for an increasing number of women who have chosen this role. Rather, they are there as psychological buffers to protect the *real* mother a little longer in the child's imaging when the child reaches the age at which a mother with cruel or self-seeking sides cannot be accommodated in the child's world-view. In this particular tale, "It is females, the step-mother and the witch, who are the inimical forces.... Gretel's importance in the children's deliverance reassures the child that a female can be a rescuer as well as a destroyer."[32] The gingerbread house or the house made of sweetmeats stands, says Bettelheim, for

> oral greediness and how attractive it is to give in to it.... But, as the story tells, such unrestrained giving in to gluttony threatens destruction. Regression to the earliest *heavenly* state of being — when on the mother's breast one lived symbiotically off her — does away with all individuation and independence. It even endangers one's very existence, as cannibalistic inclinations are given body in the figure of the witch.[33]

The opera *Hansel and Gretel*, by Engelbert Humperdinck (1854-1921), has been described as perhaps the only fine work in the operatic repertory to which one can take a child with the definite certainty of gratitude. In it, the mother and father are simply that. The children are scolded by their mother for laziness, a jug of milk is upset and the children are sent off to pick wild strawberries in the wood — up to this point, an everyday domestic scene. Father is aghast when he finds out later — he knows of an ogress in the wood — and the father and mother rush off to seek the children. Again, not much is untoward. Hansel and Gretel gather a good many strawberries (which Hansel absent-mindedly consumes), the children lose their way, say their prayers and go to sleep. A simpler age. It is worth noting that the libretto was written by Adelheid Wette, the composer's sister, who is rarely mentioned and never gets her name in bold print. The music and lyrics are enchanting. Gretel is referred to as "clever Gretel," and, to the strains of a memorable chant, the death of the witch and the freeing of many other children is celebrated: Gretel, the liberator, has slain the forces of darkness.

Unlike the ill-fated babes in the woods, the Humperdinck and Wette Hansel and Gretel are protected by their innocence: "fourteen angels watch to keep," including "two to whom 'tis given to guide their steps to heaven." This lullaby reminds the audience that spending the night in the woods is no mean feat, but it also assures us that a mantle of innocence has magic powers of protection — the children need fear no evil.

Gretel, a sweet and pretty girl, is capable of great cunning and duplicity when she decides to rebel. She succeeds in outwitting the witch, saving lives, and carrying home the witch's hoard to her impoverished family. No longer an economic liability, she is a decided asset. Gretel lies to the witch and persuades Hansel to offer a skinny stick or bone rather than a nicely rounded finger between the bars of the cage in which he spends the bulk of the story —all the better to deceive that short-sighted incarnation of evil. Perhaps most interesting of all, Gretel feigns stupidity. Having heated the oven (to cook herself or Hansel — versions differ), she persuades the witch to test the temperature. Then it's up with her heels, smother her squeals, and into the oven she goes! With great dispatch, Gretel unlocks Hansel's cage, appropriates the witch's treasure and heads for home. There she and Hansel find a contrite and lonely father (if the witch was really a transmutation of the step-mother), a grieving father and a reformed step-mother, or two relieved but rejoicing parents — in any case, a family to be going on with.

It is wise to be lenient towards Hansel. Eating wild strawberries and forgetting that birds eat bread crumbs scarcely constitute major transgressions. He is co-operative, to be sure. Children working together for their own salvation and economic independence heralds, in Bettelheim's view, the outgrowing of immature dependence on parents and the attainment of the next stage of development: "cherishing also the support of age-mates."[34]

Gretel emerges as the existential and unsung female of fairy-tale and clearly requires applause. Sharing the laurels with Hansel while he kept his hands clean has relegated her to a position of unbecoming modesty from which the contemporary reader may rescue her without delay.

LITTLE WOMEN
by
LOUISA MAY ALCOTT

We may well question the reasons for the perennial popularity of *Little Women*. It is dated and sentimental and full of preaching and moralizing, yet two things keep it alive and well and living. First of all, the little women are jealous, mean, silly and lazy and, as Elizabeth Janeway remarks "for well over a hundred years jealous, mean, silly and lazy girls have been ardently grateful for the chance to read about themselves."[35] In the second place, the irony in *Little Women* lifts it out of Victorian times and places it squarely in the life of every young woman.

> Jo is the one women in nineteenth century fiction who maintains her individual independence, who gives up no part of her autonomy as payment for being born a woman and who gets away with it. Jo is the tomboy dream come true, the dream of growing up into full humanity with all its potentialities instead of into limited femininity: of looking after oneself and paying one's way and doing

effective work in the real world instead of learning how to please a man who will look after you, as Meg and Amy both do with pious pleasure.

It is worth noting that the other two adored nineteenth century heroines who say *No* to the hero's proposal, but who give way in the end, when circumstances and the hero have changed are Elizabeth Bennet and Jane Eyre. But Jo says *No* and does not shift.[36]

Jo is a tomboy but never a masculinized or lesbian figure. She is, somehow, an idealized *New Woman*, capable of male virtues but not, as the Victorians would have said *unsexed*. Or perhaps she is really archaic woman, recreated out of some New World frontier necessity when patriarchy breaks down.[37]

In any case, "this Victorian moral tract, sentimental and preachy, was written by a secret rebel against the order of the world, and woman's place in it," and thanks to its ironic innuendoes, "all the girls who ever read it know it."[38]

This may be too inclusive a statement, the vagaries of reader-response being what they are, but when twentieth-century women are asked about female characters in fiction who influenced them, more often than not Jo March leads the parade. A moral tract, sentimental and preachy it is, to be sure, but *Little Women* is also a rousing good story about women and girls managing on their own, and one girl resolutely marching to her own drummer. There is little evidence that children are bothered by either the preachy or the sentimental elements in *Little Women*. They don't even seem to mind the frequent entreaties to the Almighty. These features are tedious or embarrassing to most adult readers, but children skip over them, lured by the seductions of plot or simply accepting that this is how people were, much as they would accept setting and habits in a tale of a remote wilderness.

The book is episodic, each chapter being structured around an event that reveals or reinforces aspects of the characters. The pressure to conform and the wonderful rewards that ensue are implicit in the pious Victorian March family household. Jo strains under its constraints and, while her antics are scarcely wild by contemporary standards, they must be viewed in their own time.

"Jo does use such slang words" observed Amy with a reproving look at the long figure stretched out on the rug. Jo immediately sat up, put her hands in her pockets, and began to whistle. "Don't, Jo: it's so boyish."

"That's why I do it."

"I detest rude, unlady-like girls."

"I hate affected, niminy-piminy chits."[39]

Jo is anything but a "niminy-piminy chit." In the absence of brothers, Jo is able to play the male parts to her heart's content when the March sisters need a Don Pedro or a Rodrigo for their home-grown dramatic productions. Many questions arise about achievement and derring-do among girls in environments without boys. The research is inconclusive, but strongly suggests that when there are no boys on which to lavish great expectations, no males to do the difficult chores or make the big decisions — no males to play male parts, as it were — then those expectations, chores, decisions and roles fall to girls, who handle them with about the same finesse and bungling as boys do. When much is expected, apparently, much may be forthcoming. When little is expected or required, only the toughest individual is likely to stretch beyond mediocrity. We are learning that the range of possibilities for both sexes is more extensive than we dreamed. While the term "tomboy" is no longer really acceptable, it took tomboys such as Jo, in life and in literature, to force the issue, and we are the beneficiaries.

> "You must have gloves, or I won't go;" cried Meg decidedly. "Gloves are more important than anything else; you can't dance without them, and if you don't I should be so mortified!"
>
> "Then I'll stay still. I don't care very much for company dancing; it's no fun to go sailing around; I like to fly about and cut capers.... Then I'll go without. I don't care what people say!" cried Jo, taking up her book.[40]

The wearing of gloves to dances is not a vital issue for most people today. It is easy to cheer for Jo's limited patience with it. We cannot, however, dismiss the concern with externals that so obsesses Meg and has its equivalent in our society.

Jo's ambition was to do "something very splendid; what it was she had no idea as yet." Most young children want to do "something very splendid" one day, yet for many adolescent girls, "doing something splendid" ceases to be a goal. We say we must be "realistic," not set our sights too high, learn to compromise. Perhaps we say this too soon; perhaps hopes are eroded too early. Perhaps we simply define doing something splendid too narrowly. For all her Victorian self-flagellation, Jo does hold herself and her hopes in high esteem. Controlling her temper and the violence she fears resides within her seems trivial beside Amy's self-absorption and pettiness. While the moral variations of the March sisters are exposed in *Little Women,* its intent is also to probe the individual interacting with society and the element of determinism which this implies. As Meg says, "People don't have fortunes left them . . . nowadays; men have to work and women marry for money. It's a dreadfully unjust world."[41]

When one considers the economic states of Hannah, the Marches and Laurie, the distribution of wealth may seem out of kilter. It is certainly immoral that "men must work for money and women must marry for it." Marriage for women becomes glorified slavery. Yet before we are too hasty in condemning this distant Victorian morality, we must ask whether attitudes towards money and marriage have fundamentally and dramatically changed. Moreover there are other points of view in *Little Women* — the March parents' marriage, for example, is far from mercenary — and double messages abound. It is wrong to care too much about money, but it is right to be frugal. Money doesn't buy happiness: the poor little rich boy next door is proof of that. While genteel poverty is exalted, gifts of grand pianos and the loan of chauffeur and carriage in emergencies make life more pleasant. Perhaps the economic and social ambivalence of the novel is best caught in the image of Jo selling her hair, her one beauty, to help her parents. She is nonchalant about it at dinner, but weeps into her pillow at night. Beauty certainly has market value, but selling it is rarely fun.

The tremendous importance of money and the confusion surrounding it are summed up in the pedantic words of Mrs. March:

Money is a good and useful thing Jo: and I hope my girls will never feel the need of it too bitterly, nor be tempted by it too much. I should like to know that John was firmly established in some good business, which gave him an income large enough to keep free from debt and make Meg comfortable. I'm not ambitious for a splendid fortune, a fashionable position, or a great name for my girls. If rank and money come with love and virtue, also, I should accept them gratefully, and enjoy your good fortune; but I know, by experience, how much genuine happiness can be had in a plain little house, where the daily bread is earned, and some privations give sweetness to the few pleasures.[42]

Money is security, money is protection from want, but money is also temptation. Good manners decreed that one not seem to care about money, and that hypocrisy be observed by all. There is no questioning of the social and economic structure: most people stay demurely in their places, in spite of Jo's rebellion.

A final word on Mrs. March, source of many virtuous speeches in the text. She may seem to be the ideal mother, but when her husband is away, as a chaplain in the civil war, she has an opportunity to be far more. With an absentee husband and a job outside the home, she is both a single parent and a working mother. She is unbelievably sweet — she *never* forgets to wave goodbye — but she is also remarkably strong. The reader is not entirely surprised, although Jo decidedly is, to learn that Mrs. March once had a violent temper. Her maturity is apparently evidenced by the complete control of her temper, and the implication is that Jo, too, will conquer her tempestuous outbursts. Another implication is that Mrs. March had been a spirited girl and, for all her middle-aged spirituality, that spirit has become strength as well as equilibrium.

Jo, very much her mother's daughter, remains a spunky role-model, a girl who kicked over enough Victorian middle-class traces (upper and lower classes have less difficulty with propriety!) to ensure that her independent outlook and behaviour will be relatively unscathed in her maturity. She says "no" to the charming rich boy and never recants. Her gumption, her temper, her warmth and good humour escape the confines of the text so that the heroine of 1868 still lives and romps today.

GONE WITH THE WIND
by
MARGARET MITCHELL

There are many readings of *Gone With the Wind* that would yield useful results; the vast injustices of slavery and inequities and iniquities of plantation life are obvious examples. A Marxist reading would show the dependence of the leisured class upon the workers, a psychological and emotional dependence as well as a dependence upon their physical work. My reading, however, will be feminist, a study of Scarlett, her position as a woman in relation to the women and men of her time, and her repeated rebellion under pressure.

Gone With the Wind, written in 1936, is, quite simply, paternalistic, racist, sexist and chauvinist. Yet it may have had more influence on the general public's perception of the American Civil War than all the documents and histories ever written. It is one of those stories that simply must be viewed in the context of its own time as well as in ours.

As we struggle toward androgynous and multi-cultural outlooks and behaviour, sexually and racially determined roles are unacceptable. Nevertheless, it is important to understand the continuing fascination of Scarlett and the moral ills of her time, which we are still attempting to outgrow. For with *Gone With the Wind,* as surely as with *Wuthering Heights* and *Dr. Zhivago*, the film version of the story cannot be ignored. While films are under no obligation to be true to the text of the novel, the film version of *Gone With the Wind*, in fact, makes a valiant effort in this direction. Girls by the thousand read the novel because they had seen the film: they delighted in recapturing something of their initial rapture because much of the dialogue was identical in both media. *Gone With the Wind* is an artefact in which the whole is greater than the sum of its parts. Deconstruction is necessary, however, for the purpose of separating manners from morality. (Ideology is so much easier to unearth from the Georgia of the Civil War than from Canada today — familiarity does not breed objectivity.)

Social and economic conditions always dictate the choices a society permits its females. The Civil War denied Scarlett the pampered privilege to be a parasite while opening up formerly unimagined possibilities for action. In a similar way, our own society, during the exigencies of war, accepted women in roles previously reserved for men, only to send them home when the bloodshed ceased.* To alter an old adage, "man's extremity has been woman's opportunity."

In an earlier but by no means simpler time, Scarlett O'Hara was forced from the elegant idleness of plantation life into everything that had been considered, only a few short months before, the exclusive domain of males. The distance from Chapter One to Chapter Thirty-Four is immense in terms of social change: Scarlett moves from indulged and coquettish irresponsibility to commitment and hardship. In Chapter One, she sits with the world at her feet in her "new green flowered muslin dress" with "its twelve yards of billowing material over her hoops." In Chapter Thirty-Four, she is decked out in green-velvet splendour. "The cock feathers gave her a dashing air and the dull green velvet of the bonnet made her eyes startling bright, almost emerald colored."[43] But between these chapters Scarlett has faced aching poverty and fatigue, and her velvet finery has been devised from rich curtains curiously out of place in the ruins of Tara. Although she appears to have gone from charming girl to splendid woman, the hands that she has forgotten to glove while the rest of her went into hiding reveal her hardship.

> Looking down she saw her own palm, saw it as it really was for the first time in a year, and a cold sinking fear gripped her. This was a stranger's palm, not Scarlett O'Hara's soft, white dimpled, helpless one. This hand was rough from work, brown with sunburn, splotched with freckles. The nails were broken and irregular, there were heavy callouses on the cushions of the palm, a half-healed blister on the thumb. The red scar which boiling fat had left last month was ugly and glaring. She looked at it in horror and, before she thought, she swiftly clenched her fist. [44]

---

*For a full analysis of this phenomenon see Ruth Pierson's book, *They're Women After All*.

Scarlett, like Morag, is an inheritor. She has inherited her Irish ancestors' love of the land, which Rhett Butler finds so misplaced. Land, to a disinherited Irish-American such as Mr. O'Hara, is of overwhelming importance. For Scarlett it becomes the extension of herself she most values, the goal worth any sacrifice. Gracious manners were placed at a high premium in pre-war Georgia and the conceptions of "lady" and "gentleman" well defined.

> What a terrible, terrible thing it was to have to do with a man who wasn't a gentleman. A gentleman always appeared to believe a lady even when he knew she was lying. That was Southern chivalry. A gentleman always obeyed the rules and said the correct things and made life easier for a lady.[45]

Many analysts of social contracts have observed that civilization is fragile at best, and that there is much to be said for codes of manners that protect us from our baser sides and from latent violence. The appellations "lady" and "gentleman" can carry connotations of the highest moral standards; they can also, of course, describe effete, ineffectual or hypocritical ways of living:

> Scarlett: "Oh, you have the nastiest way of making virtues sound so stupid."
> Rhett: "But virtues are stupid....Until you've lost your reputation, you never realize what a burden it was or what freedom really is....Always providing you have enough courage — or money — you can do without a reputation."[46]

These pronouncements are not issuing from Olympus but from that swashbuckling renegade Rhett Butler, whose attractive and infectious zest for life is one with his contempt for conventional morality: even in prison, he manages to make his own rules. In the end, however, under the influence of paternity, he learns to care very much for convention and for social acceptance. He even begins to value the family pedigree so dear to Southern hearts. Strange and unfathomable the effects of parenthood!

Belle is Rhett's long-time mistress and owner of an establishment for the practice of the oldest profession. As one in a long line of prostitutes with a heart of gold, she represents one convention at least as surely as she shuns another. (The three women, Belle the beauty, Scarlett the colorful, Melanie the sombre, would — names, manners, morals and all — provide a fertile area of examination for all those intrigued by Robert Graves and the triple female character his theories postulate.)

Melanie is, throughout the novel, a foil for Scarlett: without her, our understanding of Scarlett would be incomplete. She is always unerringly sweet and self-effacing, forever interpreting Scarlett's self-absorbtion in a generous manner, and supporting Scarlett even against family and friends who are dear to her. (Some readers are as irked by Melanie as Scarlett repeatedly is. Others find her the fixed star in a morally bankrupt galaxy. The difficulty of portraying the good in a lively manner remains the artist's problem when fallen mortals comprise the audience.) Melanie is what she seems. Scarlett has spirit and spunk in large measure, and as she moves from riches to rags, clinging fiercely to her pride and her land, we admire her. She is indomitable woman determined to survive. While not the most tender of creatures, her very toughness is what the hour demands. Children must be born and fed, the old and confused cared for. Her brand of "practicality of flesh and spirit" keeps not only herself but the residents of her beloved Tara — quite literally — alive.

The war and the cause of winning is omnipresent. Abe Lincoln is a villain and every Yankee a damned one. The inevitability of the outcome does little to lessen the reader's sense of what the South was going through. Rhett knows that you can make as much money from the wreckage of a civilization as from its construction. Opportunists are always with us. While women have waged war and men have been confirmed pacifists, most societies encourage their males to be more pugilistic than their females. Scarlett's dismissal of war is vapid, but no more stereotyped than the response of the boys. The last thing they appear to crave is the comradeship of women.

> "If you say *war* just once more, I'll go in the house and shut the door. I've never gotten so tired of any one word in my life as *war* unless it's *secession*." The boys were enchanted, as she had intended them to be, and they hastened to apologize for boring her. They thought none the less of her for her lack of interest. Indeed, they

thought more. War was men's business, not ladies' and they took her attitude as evidence of femininity.[47]

Eventually, of course, Scarlett is dragged into an intense interest in some aspects of the war. She knows that she and Frank are on the Yankees' black list and lives in constant fear. "No one in Atlanta could have loathed the Yankees more than she did, for the very sight of a blue uniform made her sick with rage."[48]

Scarlett uses others as means to her own ends, but often the very lives of family and friends depend upon her selfish tenacity. Scarlett plots and schemes, but the last thing she wants to be is introspective. The past is something she strives valiantly to forget. She uses the procrastinator's refrain, "I'll think about that tomorrow," and when even the strong shoulders she is proud of are over-burdened, this attitude is her salvation. In fact, she always does something — something almost always rebellious — under pressure.

The strictures of a society in which widows must wear black and refuse to dance and in which "no lady ever showed herself when she was pregnant" did everything to keep women in a stifled state. Scarlett, who was eager to live out loud, was silenced and curbed and thwarted. She scandalized Atlanta by running a sawmill and by going about the streets obviously pregnant. In the first instance, she is damned for doing a man's job; in the second, for doing a woman's.

Scarlett used her gracious Southern manners to charm the Yankee officers. By treating them more warmly than anyone else did, she was assured of sales of her lumber. Business is business, we say, as if the usual standards of morality were suspended in commercial matters. (Service industries, such as restaurants and bars, have no misgivings about using female charm to sell their products, and visual advertising of all sorts has found that feminine pulchritude sells everything from cars to headache medicine.) Before we condemn Scarlett for using whatever currency came to hand, we need to examine the business ethics of our own culture. How much moral progress have we really made?

Aunt Pauline and Aunt Eulalie sit in judgement upon Scarlett for being unwomanly when she attends to mills and book-keeping. Scarlett reflects upon their accusations: "Unwomanly? By God, if she hadn't been unwomanly, Aunt Pauline and Aunt Eulalie wouldn't have a roof over their heads this very minute!"[49] As Melanie points out, many of the gossips who attack Scarlett are jealous because she is "so smart and so successful...has succeeded where lots of men, even, have failed....People don't understand and people can't bear for women to be smart."[50] Aye, there's the rub. Scarlett has transgressed and conquered that no-woman's land where "lots of men, even, have failed," and the world cannot forgive this transgression.

The deception and self-deception of *Gone With the Wind* produces, among other things, a page-turner. As they work at cross-purposes, the timing between Scarlett and Rhett rivals that of Romeo and Juliet. Scarlett, who "slenderly knows herself," is driven and, not surprisingly, when she has temporarily run amok, is even driven by conscience. It "could still rise up, an active Catholic conscience."[51] Added to her other burdens is the load of guilt from which Scarlett longs to free herself. Melanie refuses to play the role of mother-confessor, believing unflinchingly in Scarlett's unassailable virtue. As Rhett predicted, the cross Scarlett will have to bear is built of Melanie's unfailing trust. Scarlett learns that confession can be tantamount to self-indulgence: "She realized that to unburden her own tortured heart would be the purest selfishness."[52] As Mitchell remarks, this is one of the few adult insights Scarlett ever has.

In spite of her lack of self-knowledge, Scarlett may be seen to acquire a deeper understanding of herself as the novel ends; or the ending may simply signal another round of the same old game. Whatever the postscript of *Gone With the Wind*, the reader must become the writer. However, we can be fairly certain that, as Mammy said of her after the death of Bonnie, Miss Scarlett will be "bearing up, same as allus." Scarlett proves herself much more than the flirtatious light-weight of the opening chapters. She becomes a woman of the hour, fighting adversity, equal to terrible pressures. Her vanity, once superficial, transforms itself into the pride of the survivor. Scarlett rebels against forces that would humiliate her or the members of her inner group. She lives through civil war: her society has gone with the wind. The more the reader considers Scarlett and her context, the more ambiguous her morality may appear.

▲

CHAPTER SIX

TOWARDS A
NEW MYTHOS

A NEW MYTHOS HERALDS NEW POSSIBILITIES and, of course, new pitfalls for women in literature and life. Are the new stories we tell reflections of new ways of thinking and living, or stories to keep up our spirits as we blaze new personal, social and political trails? One thing is certain: they have their roots in earlier stories. Long before Ruth chose to follow Naomi to another land, women were searching for ways to learn who they were, in and of themselves and in relation to other people. A new mythos will not make life easy. If, as Christine Delphy suggests, women constitute a class, their struggle need not be for ascendancy but for their own place in the sun — the as yet unclaimed birthright of all humankind. Female struggles for liberation of ideology, movement and potential are often remarkably free of enslavement of the *other* partly because difference, in feminist terms, need not imply opposition. In fact, "opposition" is either entirely absent from books in this chapter, or is vigorously opposed.

Who Do You Think You Are? is, as its title suggests, a series of questions. If we are not all going to die young and beautiful as victims of tuberculosis, mismanaged childbirth or broken hearts, and if we refuse to dwindle into wives if we do marry, we had better find out who we think we are and get on with living out loud. We had also better learn all we can about bonding and mutual support. The enemies are deep cultural feelings of inferiority, fears of both success and failure, fears of exposure and ridicule and a fear that we will loathe the self-knowledge we find. Dependency — for material security, status and identity — puts our very selves at risk. However, we risk isolation and falling flat on our faces if we venture too far. Rooms of our own and the requisite number of pounds per year are difficult to come by. All these fears are felt by Alice Munro's Rose, as she leaves Hanratty and leaves her husband in search of her self and her self-respect. Her story is a contemporary one — the female juggler keeping aloft parents, children, work, friends and lovers. Nevertheless, many of the conflicts and doubts she experiences are old as humanity. Both Morag (see Chapter Five) and Rose have a strong sense of family, but family can now be understood in different ways. Ties are no less strong because they bind different forms and structures. New stories need to come in new shapes.

Tatterhood is an old folk tale revisited, in which the value of appearance, of image, of the surface is questioned. Our society has deafened itself by looking. We are so obsessed by the visual that our ability to hear human voices, cries and music has all but atrophied. Tatterhood looks a mess. She is also capable and spirited, and the prince enjoys talking with her as he rides on his fine steed and she straddles her goat. The flattery and threat implicit in visual advertising are sharply challenged by Tatterhood, her beautiful sister and their happy friendship. Some versions of the tale have ambiguous endings in which the reader is invited to participate. Others, perversions really, show Tatterhood to have been in disguise and, like Cinderella, to have been a physical beauty after all. The reader cannot be too alert to the tendency of folk tales to comply with prevailing ideologies.

For many women, Margaret Atwood's *Surfacing* is the benchmark: their own deeply felt but repressed feminism surfaced after encountering it. Despair in the knowledge that things must stay the same the more they change is sustained. The past is powerful and we must deal with it personally and culturally to empower ourselves. Denial of the roots that clutch is ultimately self-denial. The necessity of the journey back in order to move forward to a new mythos of self and soul is at the centre of *Surfacing*. Exciting possibilities appear when we recognize that the past in Hanratty or Manawaka that we sought to escape is, like our childhood itself, a source of great strength and creativity. A recent book about women's stories and spiritual quests is appropriately titled

Diving Deep and Surfacing: one precedes the other and the potency of watery image and metaphor is effective. While we are pushed under again and again, it is to no small degree our own choice — to drown or to surface. False stories to cover pain can be overcome by the acceptance of pain and the true stories it engenders.

Maurice Sendak's *Higglety, Pigglety Pop* is a story ostensibly about a little dog with a difference. Jennie, like many women, "had everything." She also realizes, in the nick of time, that "there must be more to life than having everything." Unceremoniously she decamps. The story is short, the feelings compressed and the wrench from security to adventure brief and bright. Jennie leaves the master who loves her, without pangs of gratitude, guilt or backward glance, an inspiration to wives and daughters caught too long in a tender trap. For many, a physical escape from confinement is necessary before one can embrace a new mythos.

Margaret Drabble's *The Gifts of War* is about another kind of enslavement — not the dependency of need, but the dependency of being needed. In this short, tight tale, "Kevin's mum," for such is her identity, has one and only one reason for living. All other gods, particularly the Prince-cum-toad, have proved false; but if motherhood has betrayed her, she is not yet aware of it. The belief that most infantilizes individuals and groups is that of male superiority: its widespread acceptance is hideous and destructive to the human spirit. Kevin, a child, is *superior* to his mum. Frances and Michael, who demonstrate for peace, are themselves driven; Michael by power and Frances by male power and masochism. This story admits no easy answers: rather it shows the old mythos worn out and morally bankrupt, and makes us long for a new one.

What the stories in this section have in common is a female hero who claims her own life with a certain gusto. She takes very seriously the adage that to be is to do. She faces situations, dares to know herself and refuses to be bound by stereotypes. These stories have the power to disturb us with dreams of new possibilities.

In Rose we meet a heroine who indeed directs us towards a new mythos.

> ...though the oppression of women is indeed a material reality, a matter of motherhood, domestic labour, job discrimination and unequal wages, it cannot be reduced to these factors: it is also a question of sexual ideology, of the ways men and women image themselves and each other in a male-dominated society, of perceptions and behaviour which range from the brutally explicit to the deeply unconscious.[1]

Who Do You Think You Are?, a book of wise and wonderful symmetry, questions the reality of chronological time. In its ten self-contained yet interwoven sections, we observe Rose moving in and out of times and spaces and "the ways men and women image themselves and each other is exposed." Flo speaks of Rose's smart-aleck behaviour, rudeness, sloppiness and conceit. Her willingness to make work for others, her lack of gratitude. She mentions Brian's innocence, Rose's corruption. "Oh, don't you think you're somebody," says Flo, and a moment later, "Who do you think you are?"[2] This expression is hurled at a little girl who not only dares to have a mind of her own but, against her own best interests, makes that mind known. What in a boy would be spirit or strength is unseemly in a girl. "Man is of course willful, tough, earthy, masterful. In her [woman] these same short-comings are those of a monster: a bitch, a slob, a ball-breaking battle-axe."[3]

The wayward Rose is subjected to royal beatings: "What other way is there to manage you?" The reader can hear the self-righteous indignation in the adult voice. Who do I think I am? Nobody, of course. Well, certainly not somebody as important as *he*! The title is increasingly effective, taking on nuances and emphasizing dilemmas as the tale unfolds.

> In Giullaume de Lorris's *Le Roman de la Rose* (ca 1237), which was translated into English by Chaucer, the Rose is seen and sought by the Lover in a dream — his dream. She is a creature of his fantasy. Enclosed in her garden, she is an aesthetic-erotic-moral-semi-religious ideal: the good and the beautiful, spiritual perfection in palpable form. By being, she inspires ennobling, enabling love.

Her whole business is to be. The story of the *Roman de la Rose* is the Lover's story; the Rose is his objective.[4]

Rose's name gives us a clue to some of the possibilities and problems that may beset a contemporary flower who must undergo transplantation. It also leads us directly into a story that is an inverted or displaced fairy tale for our time. All the ancient ingredients that predate de Lorris and Chaucer are there. Rose, Briar Rose, Rose Red, are popular names for fairy-tale heroines. That the names are impersonal, not unique, universalizes the heroines' plight. Munro exploits these universal implications in an individual who stands alone and simultaneously stands for her kind.

The step mother figure, the ineffectual father, whose majesty consists in administering "royal beatings," the rich prince who can rescue the princess from poverty, humble beginnings, hard work — such things form the scaffolding of *Who Do You Think You Are?* Rose, trailing after her all the Roses of literature, makes it new. She passes through the stages of the heroine of fairy tale, working to placate the step mother who favours her natural child. Her clothes are those of the peasant child (in this case, limp corduroy with "no revelations of the figure"), destined to rise to affluence and power through the social and economic mobility only a prince can offer. "From places like West Hanratty girls move up more easily than boys."[5]

There are many female foils for Rose. Franny had been smashed when she was a baby (opinions differed as to the cause).

> Her face had got the worst of it. Her nose was crooked, making every breath she took a long, dismal-sounding snuffle. Her teeth were badly bunched together, so that she could not close her mouth and never could contain her quantities of spit. She was white, bony, shuffling, fearful, like an old woman. Marooned in Grade Two.[6]

One had to reject her immediately or she would attach herself to you. She became pregnant. She was sent away several times, until pneumonia rescued her from her fate worse than death.

Cora, of the satin dresses and glossy cosmetics, is for a time Rose's ideal.

> Rose walked around the yard behind the store, imagining the fleshy satin rippling over her own hips, her own hair rolled and dipping, her lips red. She wanted to grow up to be exactly like Cora. She did not want to wait to grow up. She wanted to be Cora, now.[7]

Cora, who turned into a big, dark, sulky-looking girl with round shoulders, is the object of Rose's first sexual stirrings, at the time when the sex of the object is incidental or accidental.

While Cora paints Rose's nails, she muses: "It's rosy to match your name. That's a pretty name, Rose. I like it."[8] Flo (who might have been a flower, too) could have been attractive, but she disguised it, dressing at thirty as if she were "fifty, sixty or even seventy." She did everything to enhance her no-nonsense approach to living, repudiating anything that might possibly be construed as vanity. Her occasional lapses into merriment give us a hint of what might have been; she drifts in the end, however, into the cage-like crib of her final years. Flo, probably the strongest single influence upon Rose, is carefully drawn. She is a cruel step-mother indeed, bringing her children up by hand, but she is more. She is the life in store for Rose unless she escapes Hanratty.

Of course, Hanratty is inescapable. Rose leaves it, goes out to dinner on it, returns to it only to leave again and for good; but Hanratty remains deep inside her — perhaps, as her reunion with Ralph Gillespie signifies, the deepest thing there.

What are the moral imperatives of Flo, Franny, Cora and the other females who populate Hanratty? Codes are strange and strict and unforgiving. Institutionalized religion, as so often happens, becomes the source or at least the focus of division and derision.

> Religion, around here, came out mostly in fights. People were Catholics or fundamentalist Protestants, honour-bound to molest each other. Many of the Protestants had been — or their families had been — Anglicans, Presbyterians. But they had got too poor to show up at those churches, so had veered off to the Salvation

Army, the Pentacostals. Others had been total heathens until they were saved. Some were heathens yet, but Protestant in fights. Flo said the Anglicans and Presbyterians were snobs and the rest were Holy Rollers, while the Catholics would put up with any two-facedness or debauching, as long as they got your money for the Pope. So Rose did not have to go to any church at all.[9]

The ironies of denominational division and their social and economic ramifications know no bounds.

The "church," however, in the form of its "clergy," does assail Rose once. "Wild Swans" is a particularly Canadian chapter of this novel, and perhaps the most brilliantly written. Flo has warned Rose to be careful of men who appear to be of the cloth and in reality are not, but she has not prepared her for the plain-clothes man who claims to be a United Church minister (Rose and the reader never know for sure). The train and the "minister's" patient hand move together in pulsating harmony. The Niagara escarpment above Dundas, the shores of Lake Ontario, the orchards of Burlington give way, just in time, to the gates and towers of the Exhibition grounds. Appearance and reality are confused at every level; but there is no mistake about Rose's participation as she travels to Toronto the Good. There is no mistake, either, that "he remained on call, so to speak, for years and years, ready to slip into place at a critical moment, without even any regard later on for husbands or lovers."[10]

Whatever inner conflict the inhabitants of the town may have experienced, the rules of home, school, street and shop in Hanratty were clear and consistent when it came to the lives of girls and women. Just as the girls and boys entered the school by different doors, so the world that awaited them within separated roles and expectations. When Rose tried to show off with her books, her father put her in her place. "Look out you don't get too smart for your own good."[11] An ideal woman, for Rose's father, and, doubtless, his townfolk, "ought to be energetic, practical, clever at making and saving; she ought to be shrewd, good at bargaining and bossing and seeing through people's pretensions. At the same time she should be naive intellectually, child-like, contemptuous of maps and long words and anything in books, full of charming jumbled notions, superstitions, traditional beliefs."[12] "Part of Rose's disgrace," she realizes, is that "she was female but mistakenly so, would not turn out to be the right kind of woman."[13]

This was, of course, prophetic. Rose tries very hard at times to be or to become the right kind of woman. Yet everywhere she goes — from university stacks, to Dr. Henshawe's house, to Patrick's parents' residence, to the maternity ward, to the Rosedale mansion — there is a different notion of the right kind of woman. Rose herself changes her ideas and ideals, sometimes in accordance with, and at other times at variance from, the prevailing winds. After hesitations and misgivings, she keeps that diamond ring, marries the heir to a substantial business and lives for a time in the right kind of house.

> I am what is around me.
> Women understand this.
> One is not a duchess
> A hundred yards from a carriage.[14]

We cheer the Roses who refuse to dwindle into wives. Yet, because they are little valued in our culture, except as wife, mother, secretary, mistress and so on, their paths are strewn with boulders and detours, not flowers: "Poverty in girls is not attractive unless combined with sweet sluttishness, stupidity. Braininess is not attractive unless combined with some signs of elegance; class. Was this true and was she foolish enough to care? It was; she was."[15] The idea that braininess casts out feminine charms persists. How far have we come from the old adage, "Be good, sweet maid, and let who will, be clever"?[16] Who do we think we are, anyway? "I thought now you was through school you'd be getting a job and help out at home."[17]

Guilt, which women are carefully conditioned to feel, regularly diminishes intellectual exhilaration and personal gratification. If the world has its way with women, all their joys, it seems, must be guilt-edged. They have what Dorothy Dinnerstein calls a "monstrously overdeveloped talent for unreciprocated empathy."[18] Some women have started to ask if this must, however, be forever the way of the world. Dr. Henshawe "liked poor girls, bright girls, but they had to be fairly good-looking girls."[19] Rose typifies the woman who, because she is reasonably bright and, more important, unmarried and unattached, can have a life, a story of her own. Unless they enter the priesthood, itself a pretty cohesive community, men have never been required to make this rigid choice between mating, progeny and domestic life and a career, job or profession — a life in the world. When Rose is considering marriage to Patrick, Dr. Henshawe asks, "But what about your studies and your degree? Are you going to forget all that so soon?"[20]

Rose and the reader get plenty of warnings that marriage to Patrick may not be the proverbial bed of roses. Patrick thinks of Rose as the White Goddess, but he clearly knows as little of Graves's book as he does of his beloved's mind and heart. He also thinks Rose looks like the Beggar Maid, "meek, voluptuous, with her shy, white feet" and "milky surrender, helplessness and gratitude."[21] Rose realizes that the swarthy, clever and barbaric king might well reduce her to this state, but Patrick clearly does not see it. Whiteness — of the goddess, of the feet of the Beggar Maid, of the serene white hands of Madame Merle or D.M. Thomas' white hotel — is a most ambiguous modifier applied to women. "Wife, sweetheart. Those mild, lovely words. How could they apply to her? It was a miracle; it was a mistake. It was what she had dreamed of, it was not what she wanted."[22]

The friendship between Jocelyn and Rose, including Rose's mischief with Jocelyn's husband, is intricately handled and asks a profound question about female identity. Jocelyn and Rose establish their friendship in a maternity ward by rebelling against the silly sweet nursery talk that sickens with its claustrophobic domesticity and unrelieved materialism. Their individual rebellions are even more significant. Jocelyn, from an upper-middle-class family, finds hard physical work, lack of money and marriage to an artist all necessary to set her apart from her family. Rose, in her rage to escape the values and limitations of Hanratty, must live for a time with a materially ambitious husband in a planned and manicured suburb. Eventually, when their energies are required for other causes, rebellion ceases to be so important for both women. The novel does seem to ask and then beg the question whether all such rebellion is illusory.

The homage due the male artist from the women in his milieu is examined unflinchingly. "Women usually aren't great artists,"[23] says the educated and unconventional Jocelyn. Munro reminds us that "these were the ideas of most well-educated, thoughtful, even unconventional or radical young women of the time."[24] Referring to the female writer, Jean-Jacques Rousseau, in an effort to explain that the *Portuguese Letters* were written by a man, declares that

> Women in general show neither appreciation nor proficiency nor genius in any part ... the celestial fire which heals and engulfs the soul, the genius which consumes and devours, that burning eloquence, those sublime raptures which transmit delight to the very foundation of the soul will always be lacking from women's writing.[25]

Perhaps "the woman," as she is called, who is doing a paper on the suicide of female artists, tiresome as she is, owes her topic — Diane Arbus, Virginia Woolfe, Sylvia Plath, Anne Sexton, Christiane Pflug — to such androcentric attitudes. This may be particularly and painfully accurate because, while men may articulate patriarchal articles of faith, women by the thousand obediently subscribe to them. They let the untalented and the intellectually and aesthetically indolent off the hook. No need to fear success or failure, of course, if you're not even obliged to play! Consideration of who the artist thinks she is is a variation on the theme of the book.

Jocelyn and Rose share a deep friendship, but as Jocelyn and Clifford become consumers of the sort Jocelyn once ridiculed and their lives become brittle and desperate, the friendship becomes strained. While Clifford differs substantially from Patrick, Jocelyn may be what Rose might have become had she decided that Patrick's wife was who she really was. Jocelyn and Clifford are, by most standards, successful; but, perched on the edge of their splendid ravine, they are dangerously close to moral bankruptcy.

Rose is our fourth and final female blessed with a single daughter. After Rose's departure, Anna initially lives with her father in the family home, in child-like fashion, to stay with her friends: later she returns to material advantage with her father and a step-mother. In the interval she and Rose live together. "Poor, picturesque, gypsying childhoods are not much favoured by children, though they will claim to value them, for all sorts of reasons, later on."[26] The time that Rose and Anna manage on their own, however, is one of poignancy and intimacy as well as fatigue and frustration for Rose. The postponed and eventually cancelled trysts with lovers are familiar to women coping with children. The planning, the disappointments, the expectancy, the guilt, the hope, the resentment, the despair are all part of the pattern. Anna gets sick, as children will when their mothers engineer get-aways. After Rose's meeting with Tim is cancelled yet again, Anna, almost recovered, tells her mother this dislocated fairy tale with its transparent symbolism:

> There was a white princess who dressed all in bride clothes and wore pearls. Swans and lambs and polar bears were her pets, and she had lilies and narcissus in her garden. She ate mashed potatoes, vanilla ice cream, shredded coconut and meringue off the top of pies. A pink princess grew roses and ate strawberries, kept flamingoes (Anna described them, could not think of the name) on a leash. The blue princess subsisted on grapes and ink. The brown princess though drably dressed feasted better than anybody; she had roast beef and gravy and chocolate cake with chocolate icing, also chocolate ice cream with chocolate fudge sauce. What was there in her garden? "Rude things," said Anna. "All over the ground."[27]

Rose's love for Simon and the sudden rightness of their brief interlude attests to Rose's resilience as well as to her need and capacity for hope and sharing. Rose is amazed that "even at this late date she could have thought herself the only person who could seriously lack power."[28] Early conditioning is seen as blocking the imagination of a deeply sensitive woman. Rose's extended drive in search of Simon, self and peace is (as is Morag's more definitive journey), an option unthinkable for heroines such as Emma, Isabel and Tess, and, indeed, is beyond most women today. Western middle-class women may not have much social, economic, vocational or political mobility but, for many, physical mobility has become a reality.

In the chapters "Spelling" and "Who Do You Think You Are," the alternative to an early death such as Simon's is depicted at the Home where the old people are arranged in tiers. Rose eventually overcomes her temptation to make fun of Flo. (As an artist, she has naturally enough made good use of the material available in Hanratty memories, from Milton to Flo.)

> What stopped her was, in fact, that gulf; she had a fresh and overwhelming realization of it, and it was nothing to laugh about. These reproaches of Flo's made as much sense as a protest about raising umbrellas, a warning against eating raisins. But they were painfully, truly, meant; they were all a hard life had to offer. Shame on a bare breast.[29]

"It is not families who care for the aged, it is women — wives and daughters." So reads the popular sociology of the daily paper. Flo's extremity is of more concern to her female step-child than to the male fruit of her loins. While the novel provides no easy answers, it requires that the reader's moral imagination strive for an aged life sweeter than a crib in a Home — a cruel mockery of life's beginning at its end. Each novelist who has her readers face age and infirmity head on, as *The Stone Angel* and *Who Do You Think You Are?*, has done us noble service.

In the character of Rose, Munro has taken a familiar name and an old, old story and re-worked it towards a new mythos — the artist, bleeding and bare-breasted if need be, as heroine. Fairy tale as structure, familiar myth as content and a brave new woman carrying the day. Rose discovers who it is she thinks she is. The only access to such self-knowledge is the flinty, upward path now grudgingly opening to women. It is to Munro's credit that she in no way underestimates the struggle or romanticizes it. She shows us more unequivocally than Virginia Woolfe in *Orlando* or Margaret Atwood in *Lady Oracle* that the ancients were right: insight and self-knowledge still come through suffering. *Woman must weep,* say song and folklore; perhaps now she is to work as well, not silently and unsung, but out loud and recognized.

Women, who have never been strangers to suffering, may, through female protagonists such as Rose, have that suffering dignified through art. Julia Kristeva recognizes "that women and certain 'revolutionary' literary works pose a radical question to existing society precisely because they mark out the frontier beyond which it dare not venture."[30] There are signs in *Who do You Think You Are?* that societal boundaries are being pushed to the breaking point.

TATTERHOOD
Edited by
ETHEL JOHNSTON PHELPS

"Tatterhood" is the title story from a collection of "old stories about magic and adventure."[31] A king and queen long for a child. Through the agency of a magic spell, their wish is granted and they are blessed with not one but two daughters. The first is a "queer looking creature" called Tatterhood; her twin is fair and sweet. Although they are different —foils for each other — the sisters love each other and, thanks to Tatterhood's sailing abilities, have wonderful adventures.

After a quest that proves her mettle, Tatterhood and her sister decide to "sail on and see something of the world." When they reach a distant kingdom they are greeted by a messenger, who invites them to the castle for an audience with the two sons of the king. Tatterhood replies with characteristic independence: "No," said Tatterhood, "Let them come down to the ship if they wish to see us."[31] Predictably, the elder son falls in love with the beautiful sister, but she is not without spunk and is in no hurry to leave Tatterhood. Because of the folk-tale convention of offering hospitality to strangers, the sisters are invited to a feast at the castle. The prince's brother is more or less stuck with Tatterhood, who makes no move to alter her appearance. "I will go as I am." While the others ride on horseback, Tatterhood rides her goat, even though she can turn it into a fine steed at will. She demonstrates magic powers, changing garments and gear in the twinkling of an eye; by now the younger prince is sufficiently captivated by the reality of Tatterhood that he no longer cares excessively about how she looks.

> When the castle loomed up ahead, Tatterhood said to him, "And will you not ask to see my face beneath the streaks of soot?" "That, too, shall be as you choose."[32]

As they rode through the castle gate, Tatterhood touched a rowan wand to her face, and the soot streaks disappeared. Whether her face was now lovely or plain we shall never know, because it didn't matter in the least to the prince or to Tatterhood.

This is a refreshing old tale, an indication that there has always been a current of what we might now call feminist thought running through our literary traditions. The importance of distinguishing between appearance and reality, between how we look and what we know and can do is ancient lore. In this story-collection we have a chance to go back to our roots, which, on occasion, do not seem to be exclusively sexist. It is helpful to remember that much of the sexism in life, art and culture that we assume to have existed since the dawn of time is actually a man-made convention. There is some cause for hope. Some lingering images are being overturned: Mrs. Noyes is rescued at last from the defamation of character ascribed her in the miracle and morality plays. She had been the prototype of the shrewish wife until Timothy Findley's *Not Wanted on the Voyage* portrayed her as a nurturing, caring woman, who includes the deformed, the maimed, the aged and the unusual in her concern.

Early works, such as folk-tales, do not necessarily view the female of the species as any more shrewish, dependent, irrational or incapable of decision and action than the male. The discovery of early versions that affirm women in their full humanity is at least as important as revisionist scholarship to women's ability to live out loud. Tatterhood is waiting to be celebrated. Such tales are morality plays, too, enabling and raising the possibility of comradeship between the sexes.

THE GIFTS OF WAR
by
MARGARET DRABBLE

Margaret Drabble is a distinguished woman of letters, the most recent editor of the *Oxford Companion to English Literature*, and an extremely able teller of tales. Her novels are, without exception, concerned with moral tensions. There could, for example, be no more fertile soil for the examination of morality than *The Needle's Eye,* in which the place of children in a contemporary woman's life is shown with deft strokes and profound humanity. In her short fiction, *The Gifts of War*, we find a "beautiful example of Drabble's ability to make the reader feel the power of the maternal instinct."[33] "None of my books is about feminism, because my belief in the necessity for justice for women (which they don't get at the moment) is so basic that I never think of using it as a subject. It is part of a whole."[34]

As in *Surfacing*, the main protagonist of *The Gifts of War* has no name, although she is "Mum" by virtue of her relationship to her son, Kevin. In her maternal passion she is Everywoman: "'You don't know anything, Mum,' he would groan, but she didn't mind his condemnations; she didn't expect to know anything, it amused her to see him behaving like a man already, affecting superiority."[35] She knew that

> he wasn't a proper man yet, he couldn't inflict true pain ... his teasing, obligatory schoolboy complaints about her cooking and her stupidity seemed to exorcise in a way those other crueler onslaughts. It was as though she said to herself: if my little boy doesn't mean it when he shouts at me, perhaps my husband doesn't either: perhaps there's no more serious offence in my bruises and my greying hair than there is in those harmless childish moans. In the child, she found a way of accepting the man: she found a way of accepting, without too much submission, her lot.[36]

With great linguistic economy, Drabble sets us the dilemma of the woman who lives for, and through, a child, and for whom the husband and father has become a necessary evil in the equation. "She never thought of the man's emotions."[37] Her role, her place, her social dignity were all forged in her commitment to her son — her dependence upon being his mother.

The event of the story centres on Kevin turning, as the strange phrase has it, eight. Mother and son banter — a convention well developed between them — in anticipation of this event. "Mum" tries to keep Kevin just enough on edge that the surprise element of his longed-for gift will not be entirely diluted. (They both know that she will produce his heart's desire at the appointed hour.)

This woman, whose two major emotions are resentment and love, takes selfish pleasure in doing things for Kevin. Her secret, kept from the condemned cattle, the sacrificial virgins was a sense of her own salvation, her redemption through her child, which gave her a kind of superior wisdom, a higher order of knowledge.

Halfway through the story we are introduced to a sub-plot that will meet the main plot by the final paragraphs. Frances Janet Ashton Hall, who has plenty of names and is looking forward to leaving for university to study economics, is enamoured of Michael Swaines. For his sake, as much as for that of the cause, she is wearing a sandwich board, parading for peace and, to some extent, enjoying the discomfiture. Frances and Michael, quite well brought up really, middle-class, articulate and childless, are doing their half-baked political best to stop the war in Vietnam and to prevent children from playing with war toys — toys such as the Desperado Destruction Machine, which Kevin has seen on the telly, for which his mum has scrimped and saved, and which he ardently desires as his birthday gift.

Countless questions are contained in this brief, poignant, painful tale. The myths of freedom and concern clash head on. The dreams of the child and the woman are at risk because of interfering do-gooders, who have all the trappings of human frailty and are concerned about a cause that has universal repercussions. "Frances knew that in their innocence they had done something dreadful to her, in the light of which those long-since ended air raids and even distant Vietnam itself were an irrelevance, a triviality."[38] Frances glimpses too late that, in her zeal, she has trodden upon another woman's dreams. Destroying a war toy was itself an act of violence against a mother simply seeking a birthday present for her son. The human propensity for joining global causes while remaining blind and insensitive to the pain before our eyes is caught and held in this haunting story. One moral imperative challenges another.

This is a tightly-told tale that implicates us all, for we are all "Mum" and we are all Michael. Perhaps the greater torment is that we are all, to some extent, Frances, who only dimly perceives the difference.

HIGGLETY, PIGGLETY POP
by
MAURICE SENDAK

This is a story about a little dog who had everything:

> Once Jennie had everything. She slept on a round pillow upstairs and a square pillow downstairs. She had her own comb and brush, two different bottles of pills, eyedrops, eardrops, a thermometer and for cold weather, a red wool sweater. There were two windows for her to look out of and two bowls to eat from. She even had a master who loved her.[39]

Jennie had everything, but "Jennie didn't care." "I am discontented. I want something I do not have. There must be more to life than having everything."[40] Jennie packs her bag in the middle of the night and heads off into the unknown. There she will be on her own, she will have to fend for herself. She joins a circus and works very hard; but there is no suggestion that she ever wants to return to the potted plant and the master who would, metaphorically, kill her with kindness.

Jennie's decisions are those that, during the next two decades, we will have to reckon and deal with in new and imaginative ways. The story is perhaps easier, and certainly less threatening, as it is about a shaggy little dog. The reader can take or leave as much of the new mythos as she likes or feels ready for. The wide world has a way of mowing us down, and leaving the security of the dog's house or the doll's house is not to be undertaken lightly.

Unlike female characters who have dependants and whose situation is, therefore, more complex, Jennie is a dependant apparently weary of dependency and anxious to strike out on her own. Jennie is the protected wife who wants to work out her own salvation. She is also the cared-for, pampered and petted female child whose master and father loves her, but not enough to let her go.

Jennie starts out with plenty of possessions — pills, pillows, cosy sweaters and thermometers. She finds, however, that our identity may rest with our adventures rather than with our possessions. We are what we know and what (in a creative, not a vocational, sense) we do. This shaggy little dog with a mission is able to provoke without anxiety a consideration of a new mythos.

SURFACING
by
MARGARET ATWOOD

In *Surfacing*, as in her other novels and poems, Margaret Atwood gives women a voice. Her work is clean and tough — of its time and place yet with universal appeal and import.*

> In fiction, there are some curious stories, such as Margaret Atwood's *Surfacing* and Marion Engel's *Bear*, of heroines turning away from their civilized heritage toward an identity with nature. It seems clear that for Canadian culture, the old imperialistic phrase "going native" has come home to roost. We are no longer an army of occupation, and the natives are ourselves.[41]

The unnamed narrator and protagonist of *Surfacing* goes on the journey back, and in, and, finally, beyond. The Canadian wilderness is the setting for the novel, "home-ground," "foreign territory," as the story teller calls it. The flat cliff reveals the usual assortment of messages,

> some faded and defaced, others fresh yellow and white. VOTEZ GODET, VOTEZ O'BRIEN ...THÉ SALADA, BLUE MOON COTTAGES 1/2 MILE, QUÉBEC LIBRE, FUCK YOU, BUVEZ COCA COLA GLACÉ, JESUS SAVES, mélange of demands and languages, an x-ray of it would be the district's entire history.[42]

---

*Margaret Atwood's *Bodily Harm* and *The Handmaid's Tale* are also excellent masques of morality.

The occasion for the return to Northern Quebec is the search for her missing father. Until now she has managed to keep thoughts of both her parents more or less at bay. "They have no right to get old."[43] She considers herself powerless and betrayed because her parents did not communicate their power to her. Her friends, facilitating and accompanying her on the physical journey and throwing into relief some of her discoveries, are embarrassed by the reason for the search: "they don't understand it. They all disowned their parents long ago, the way you are supposed to: Joe never mentions his mother and father, Anna says hers were nothing people and David calls his The Pigs."[44]

The admonition about homecoming applies: "You can never go home." She can't, because so much has changed; yet she can, because so many things — such as the bottle house and Paul — are still there. Finally she must, if she is to come to terms with her parents, her self and her lost capacity for feeling; she must return and "know the place for the first time." The accumulated details of the journey in — from ice-cream cones served in a new way to the play and pretending of childhood — work to bring the past into uncomfortably sharp focus. Skilful descriptions of photographs invoke the past; but they, like word stories, are only the photographer's and viewer's versions. In order to contact our own pasts we must connect, however tenuously, with the time before we were. The protagonist finally can see a frog as her ancestor and the dead heron as a symbol of death and renewed life. "Grandmothers and grandfathers first, distant ancestors, in face-front firing squad poses.... My mother before she was married, another stranger, with bobbed hair and a knitted hat. Wedding pictures, corseted smiles. My brother before I was born, then pictures of me begin to appear."[45] Part of getting back to nature is getting back to our own human nature. In this case, our father's mind and our mother's body herald, at first, the usual sexual resonances, and a hackneyed strain seems to enter an otherwise quick and invigorating melody. When one reflects, however, upon how important the body is in *Surfacing*, the strength imparted from mother to daughter can be staggering.

The importance of food, the importance of death to life is relentlessly insisted upon.

> Blocked feelings do not go away; they fester inside...her ability to accept the painful truth about the past counteracts the anaesthesia, abolishes the need for false stories to cover up true pain. By allowing herself to feel pain, she unblocks her feelings and contacts her energy and power....[46] Feeling was beginning to seep back into me, I tingled like a foot that's been asleep.[47]

Actually, the protagonist has always been very interested in power but never admitted her complicity with it. Now that she no longer hides behind feigned innocence and the illusion that she is helpless — two common female blocks to wholeness — she regains her capacity for feeling. "Atwood has done more than nostalgically recall an ancient world view. She has suggested a direction for the transformation of modern consciousness that would be beneficial for women and all life."[48]

The protagonist's first pregnancy and her abortion were not her choices. Now she chooses to become pregnant. She is no longer a victim of gender or of male attitudes. Our past is made up of the stories we weave and tell and reinforce about it. The protagonist recognizes that she needs a new version of her story. She is "allowing her own feelings, not male *morality* to define reality for her."[49] She has looked into the heart of nature and can deal, as all humanity must, with ancestors and progeny. Referring to her parents, she says, "To prefer life, I owe them that."[50] When one decides to steer one's own course rather than to drift, the power of one's ancestors and one's own power become accessible.

To move towards a new mythos is costly and risky, but the costs and risks of staying mired in the mud of patriarchy are much greater. Many thoughtful women and men are now trying alone and together to move towards new ways of acting and being. Old values need to be rethought, reworked and sometimes even discarded, for such, in Alice Munro's poignant phrase, is "the progress of love."*

---

*Alice Munro's *The Progress of Love* (1986) is a splendid collection of short fiction.

▲

AFTERWORD

In *Masques of Morality*, we have looked steadfastly at females in fiction and in life. It remains to reckon where we think we are and to reconcile past, present and an array of possible futures. If we are to escape the terrifying, perhaps prophetic, vision of *The Handmaid's Tale* we will need to construct and tell new stories of our own very soon.

Many women, after all, are still protected, pampered pets denied and denying an individual identity. Often they are accomplished consumers who produce almost nothing. Their striving and their good works go unrecognized and unsung, stifled by patriarchy. They remain in dead marriages, dead-end jobs, or are themselves simply deadened, by their dependence upon males. The rewards of promotion in the work-place and the social comfort of the Saturday-night date have by no means exhausted themselves as powerful motivation. By squinting ever so slightly one can glimpse Emma, in the return of the ostentatious formal wedding, borne on the possessive arm of Mr. Woodhouse until summarily transferred to the arm of Mr. Knightly — charming, living, breathing private property.

Women are still despised and rejected for their very nature, which is adored and feared simultaneously. They are seen as temptresses who must be condemned because mere men have no power to resist them. That such a view of the relationship between the sexes is as demeaning to males as to females is crystal clear. We are now likely to loathe the twentieth-century version of Angel Clare yet continue the ritualistic purge and metaphorical murder of the contemporary Tess.

Isabel, the heiress, is living, "and partly living", in every upper-middle-class ghetto in the country. If you observe carefully on a mellow autumn afternoon, you may just catch sight of Osmond, hand-in-hand with Pansy. Although Pansy, one hundred years later, is still a bit afraid, they walk together most agreeably. Isabel, within, could pose convincingly for the glossy magazine, table luxuriously furnished (often through the services of another woman), serene in her perfect understated black, candles lit, the ironic masque about to begin.

Morag is everywhere among us, at every stage of her life, hanging on to her "shit" in her particular Manawaka, marrying Brooke and living "properly" for a time, committing some act of wilful wildness without which she cannot trust herself to wrench free from the considerable comforts of the empty marriage nest. In the end, she earns not only her bread but her space — the green world accessible only at great cost and only to the mature woman.

While Rose's masque is that of a contemporary hero, her sisters from all the previous chapters are living in her time, our time. Her story offers hope that we can somehow keep alive the never resolved, perhaps never resolvable, tension between caring for others and caring for ourselves. Rose is a part of all the children, women, men, work and wonder of her life, but more significantly she is *Rose*, much greater than the sum of these parts. She is both remarkably strong and touchingly vulnerable. Her conflicts, with their ancient echoes, are the particular conflicts of her time, her place, her situation, her sex and herself. Rose's consciousness of who she is comes to her in a direct line from narrative, the combined stories she tells herself about life and its meaning, the stories she engenders in those whose lives she touches and the communal stories that she struggles to grasp and to change.

"The bias of art is still to see truth in the rich particular rather than in the lowest common denominator of a hundred case histories."[1] It is this "rich particular" within women's stories that we have sought throughout this book. Our stories are being told, our souls becoming known. The power of the female narrative, from Emma's story to the saga of the unnamed hero of *Surfacing*, demonstrates that "insight into the complexities of life is still, for all the 'scientific' studies, the province of literature."[2]

▲

APPENDIX

> Writers and audience are Siamese twins. Kill one and you run the
> risk of killing the other. Try to separate them and you may simply
> have two dead half-people.[1]

Since nobody can be certain which text will fit best with which
reader at which time and in which circumstances, I am suggesting
fifty additional masques of morality, ten related to each theme.
The reader may choose to add texts that seem to belong or to
connect in some way with those I have listed: I hope this is what
happens. I would be grateful to hear of texts that seem to other
readers particularly apt in any of the five groupings I have
identified.

> ...the mask metaphor fails us if it assumes that there is a real me
> underneath the mask I put on. There is no core to that onion: there
> is never anything underneath a persona except another persona.
> When we are alone we have not walked away from a theatrical
> situation, we have walked into another one of a different
> kind....Within everyone there dwells an entire Ottawa of politicians
> jockeying for power; civil servants struggling with routine, mass
> demonstrators organizing temper tantrums, secretaries trying to
> transcribe the inner turmoil into some kind of self-justifying
> narrative.[2]

Of course, one might as easily say an entire London, Washington,
Tokyo or Paris: Canadians are not alone in their ability to
accommodate a dozen or more masks in the head. It appears that
texts are not only subjected to different readers' reading through
time and space, but that a number of different readers may dwell
at any time within a single person. It is to be expected, then, that
given certain readers' readings of the texts I have mentioned,
these texts will be seen to belong in different spots. Again, this is
as it should be, and again I would welcome collaboration.

CHAPTER TWO
WHAT IS TO BE DONE?

As we have observed, this is a question that is still going strong in many contexts: it is appropriate, therefore, to range about in the selection of additional texts. *Esther Waters, Middlemarch, The Odd Woman* and *Wuthering Heights* are masques of morality written by women and men whose imaginations were troubled by woman's position in the scheme of things. *Its Image on the Mirror, The Doll Maker* and *Bird at the Window*, each using a metaphor now familiar in language about women, provide modern instances‚ of the recognition of the need for change, combined, at times, with a measure of uncertainty as to which move to make next. *Unleaving* concerns the pain and exhilaration of growing up and, like many so-called "adolescent novels," is nourishing fare for any age. While *The Tin-Lined Trunk* and *The Root Cellar* are novels enjoyed by younger readers, a reading shared among the generations is likely to lend richness to the experience. Only by collapsing boundaries and distinctions among us, including those of age, will we ever decide, in any comprehensive way, what is to be done.

> *Esther Waters* by George Moore
> *Unleaving* by Jill Paton Walsh
> *Its Image on the Mirror* by Mavis Gallant
> *Middlemarch* by George Eliot
> *Wuthering Heights* by Emily Bronte
> *The Odd Woman* by George Gissing
> *The Tin-Lined Trunk* by Ron Berg
> *The Root Cellar* by Janet Lunn
> *Bird at the Window* by Jan Truss
> *The Dollmaker* by Harriette Arnow

CHAPTER THREE

CAN ANYTHING BE DONE?

It is likely that the kindred masques in this section will be of use for the contemporary reader only when scrutinized from a feminist perspective. The "hopeless cases" in such stories as *The Yellow Wallpaper*, *The Bell Jar* and *Polarities*, all declared insane by the conventional wisdom of their time, may be seen as the only characters with a shred of sanity in their topsy-turvy worlds of male assumptions and presumptions. While Tess dies for attempting to murder the situation in which she is caught, and while Hester must ascend the scaffold, women may also be declared imbalanced, strange, misfits or simply insane because they have questioned the prevailing order. The heavy weight of determinism and an oppressive lack of choice characterize to some extent all the texts in this additional list: they echo with the irony of *Sophie's Choice*. While the fates of the characters in stories such as *Three Lives* and *The Peace of Utrecht* may seem to lie as much in themselves as in their stars, the conditioning and constraints that have moulded them reveal the odds very hard to beat.

> *Three Lives* by Gertrude Stein
> *The Awakening* by Kate Chopin
> *Sophie's Choice* by William Styron
> *The Yellow Wallpaper* by Charlotte Gilman
> *The L-Shaped Room* by Lynne Banks
> *Revelation* by Flannery O'Connor
> *The Bell Jar* by Sylvia Plath
> *Wilde Sargasso* by Jean Rhys
> *Polarities* by Margaret Atwood
> *The Peace of Utrecht* by Alice Munro

CHAPTER FOUR

GRACE UNDER PRESSURE

As we have noted, this cluster of texts is the most difficult to redeem in the esteem of the contemporary reader. When examining *Obasan*, *Port after Port*, *Heidi* and *The Hundred Penny Box*, for example, we may be assisted not only by the distinction Carol Gilligan and others make between the moral reasoning of females and males, but more significantly by Gilligan's observations about these distinctions. She points out that the female approach, which accents social relationships, has been widely misunderstood and devalued, while the male approach, which accents autonomy, has been considered the correct one.[3]

As Janette Turner Hospital says of Doris in *Port after Port*, "she found it difficult to shed the habit of instinctive peace-making."[4] The reader may ask if this is a habit we should always strive to shed. No principal female character in these additional masques, from *Frost in May* to *The Old Maid*, is weak or obsequious. Rather, each restores to grace something of its ancient meaning and suggests that what the macho world needs now may be to emulate this unfashionable quality.

> *From Anna* by Jean Little
> *Frost in May* by Antonia White
> *The Hundred Penny Box* by Sharon Bell Mathis
> *Heidi* by Johanna Spyri
> *The Old Maid* by Edith Wharton
> *The Eyes of the Amaryllis* by Natalie Babbitt
> *Moving* by Meguido Zola
> *Rain and I* by Dorris Heffron
> *Obasan* by Joy Kogawa
> *Port after Port, The Same Baggage* by Janette Turner
>   Hospital

CHAPTER FIVE

REBELLION UNDER PRESSURE

This group of masques of morality may be the one most easily augmented: it was certainly the most difficult for me to limit to ten additional texts. In literature written in or about any historical period and adopted by any age or group of readers, there are always a significant number of females such as Kit Tyler in *The Witch of Blackbird Pond* or Julilly and Liza in *Underground to Canada* who refuse to fit in or, as the case may be, cave in, when the pressure or the heat becomes unendurable. The hero may be six years old as in *Pandora*, twelve as in *Julie of the Wolves*, or forty-two and near death, as Deborah in *The Satellites*, but she does not view her lot as unavoidable or inescapable. Her rebellion may be reflective and silent or action-packed and loudly articulated, but it unfailingly questions the status quo. The female leads in *Jacob Have I Loved* and *Weeds* are not entirely exceptional. On one level they are, of course, hardy individuals, but on another they are typical of social ground swells — rebellion issuing from human pain and a refusal to be victims of any form of oppression.

> *The Satellites* by Gabrielle Roy
> *Tirra Lirra By the River* by Jessica Anderson
> *Jacob Have I Loved* by Katherine Paterson
> *Weeds* by Edith Summers Kelley
> *The Witch of Blackbird Pond* by Elizabeth George
>   Speare
> *Pandora* by Sylvia Fraser
> *Underground to Canada* by Barbara Smucker
> *Julie of the Wolves* by Jean Craighead George
> *The French Lieutenant's Woman* by John Fowles
> *Roll of Thunder, Hear My Cry* by Mildred Taylor

CHAPTER SIX

TOWARDS A NEW MYTHOS

The masques of morality added to this section may serve to reinforce the sense of what Thomas Kuhn has identified as a paradigm shift.[5] As our female stories remind us, we can never take for granted that such a shift has really occurred, or that it has sufficient momentum and staying power to help us. All the machinery of society, politics, economics and tame art remains in place to smother and stamp out a new mythos. Nevertheless, we are shaping new stories with new expectations, new problems and new hope. Many contemporary novels and films work towards this new mythos and, as we noted, its genesis can be found in ancient stories generating power and receiving renewed and revised attention. Thus we add *The Skull in the Snow and Other Folk Tales*, and look anew instead of askance at *Pippi Longstocking*. *All Passion Spent* and *Meridian* provide models by which to change our standard stories. *Happy Endings Are All Alike* is a moving novel intended for adolescents, but important reading for any age or sex. Together with *Invention for Shelagh*, it depicts lesbian love and caring as able, in Jane Austen's phrase, to live out loud. *Subversive Elements, Seductions of the Minotaur* and *The Shaman's Daughter* ask questions that demand responses.

> *The Female Man* by Joanna Russ
> *Subversive Elements* by Donna Smythe
> *Invention for Shelagh* by Jane Rule
> *Meridian* by Alice Walker
> *Happy Endings Are All Alike* by Sandra Scappettone
> *All Passion Spent* by Vita Sackville-West
> *Pippi Longstocking* by Astrid Lindgren
> *Seduction of the Minotaur* by Anais Nin
> *The Skull in the Snow and Other Folk Tales* by Toni
>   McCarty
> *The Shaman's Daughter* by Nan S. Salerno and
>   Rosamond M. Vanderburg

▲

RELATED READINGS

A. LITERARY CRITICISM - GENERAL

The Pleasure of the Text by Roland Barthes

On Deconstruction by Jonathan Culler

Against the Grain by Terry Eagleton

The Function of Criticism by Terry Eagleton

The Role of the Reader by Umberto Eco

Beyond Structuralism and Hermeneutics by Michel Foucault

The Archeology of Knowledge and the Discourse of Language
by Michel Foucault

Lyric Poetry: Beyond New Criticism by Chaviva Hosek and
Patricia Parker

Desire in Language: a Semiotic Approach to Literature and Art
by Julia Kristeva

Displacement: Derrida and After edited by Mark Krupnick

Semiotics and Interpretation by Robert Scholes

The Invented Reality by Paul Watzlawick

Literary Meaning: From Phenomenology to Deconstruction
by William Ray

B. FEMINIST LITERARY CRITICISM

Writing and Sexual Difference edited by Elizabeth Abel

Writing Woman: Women Writers and Women in Literature, Medieval to Modern by Sheila Delany

Feminist Literary Criticism edited by Josephine Donovan

Writing Beyond the Ending: Narrative Strategies of Twentieth Century Women Writers by Rachel Blau Du Plessis

Gender and Reading: Essays on Readers, Texts and Contexts edited by Elizabeth Flynn and Patrocinio Schweickart

Victorian Women's Fiction: Marriage, Freedom and the Individual by Shirley Foster

The Representation of Women in Fiction edited by Carolyn Heilbrun and Margaret Higonnet

Crossing the Double-Cross: The Practice of Feminine Criticism by Elizabeth Meese

Sexual Textual Politics: Feminist Literary Theory by Toril Moi

Feminist Criticism and Social Change: Sex, Class and Race in Literature and Culture edited by Judith Newton and Deborah Rosenfelt

Silences by Tillie Olsen

Archetypal Patterns in Women's Fiction by Annis Pratt

Lesbian Images by Jane Rule

Feminist Literary Studies by K.K. Ruthven

The New Feminist Criticism: Essays on Women, Literature and Theory by Elaine Showalter

Gender and Literary Voice edited by Janet Todd

C. FEMINIST THOUGHT, LANGUAGE AND EDUCATION

Women's Oppression Today by Michele Barrett

New Lesbian Writing edited by Margaret Cruikshank

The Weaker Vessel: Women's Lot in Seventeenth Century England by Antonia Fraser

In a Different Voice by Carol Gilligan

Private Woman, Public Stage by Mary Kelly

Women and Language in Literature and Society edited by Sally McConnell-Ginet, Ruth Borker and Nelly Furman

The Skeptical Feminist by Janet Radcliffe Richards

Women, Culture and Society edited by M.Z. Rosaldo and L. Lamohere

Feminist Theorists edited by Dale Spender

Man Made Language by Dale Spender

Breaking Out: Feminist Consciousness and Feminist Research by Liz Stanley and Sue Wise

Fairy Tales and the Female Imagination by Jennifer Waelti-Walters

Women's Ways of Knowing by Mary Field Belenky, Blythe McVicker Clinchy, Nancy Rule Goldberger and Jill Matluck Tarule

The Politics of Reproduction by Mary O'Brien

▲

NOTES

PREFACE

1. Robert Baker, "'Pricks' and 'Chicks': A Plea for Persons" in *Sexist Language: A Modern Philosophical Analysis*, ed. Mary Veiterling (New York: Braggins, 1966), p. 166.
2. Jane Miller, *Women Writing About Men* (New York: Pantheon, 1987).
3. Robert Scholes, *Textual Power* (New Haven: Yale University Press, 1985), p. xi.
4. Northrop Frye, "Expanding the Boundaries of Literature". Unpublished lecture in the *Mind and Matter Series*, Victoria College, 1983.
5. Annette Kolodny, "Some Notes on Defining a Feminist Literary Criticism," *Critical Inquiry*, Vol. 2 (1975), p. 77.
6. Nina Auerbach, *Romantic Imprisonment: Women and Other Glorified Outcasts* (New York: Columbia University Press, 1985), p. 84.
7. Elizabeth Meese, *Crossing the Double Cross*, (Chapel Hill: University of North Carolina Press, 1986), p. 99.
8. Rosemary Sullivan, *Stories by Canadian Women* (Toronto: Oxford University Press, 1984), p. x.
9. Jane Marcus, "Thinking Back Through Our Mothers" in *New Feminist Essays on Virginia Woolf*, edited by Jane Marcus (Lincoln: University of Nebraska Press, 1981).

CHAPTER ONE

1. Jane Austen, *Pride and Prejudice* (Harmondsworth: Penguin, 1972), p.51.
2. Gayatri Spivak, Forward to "Draupodi" in *Writing and Sexual Process*, edited by Elizabeth Abel (Chicago: University of Chicago Press, 1982), pp. 262-263.
3. Toril Moi, *Sexual Textual Politics* (New York: Methuen, 1985), p. 108.

4. Dorin Schumacher, "Subjectivities: A Theory of the Critical Process" in *Feminist Literary Criticism*, edited by Josephine Donovan (Lexington: University of Kentucky Press, 1975), p. 36.

5. Jacques Derrida, "Living on Border Lines" in *Deconstruction and Criticism*, edited by Harold Bloom (New York: Seabury, 1979), p. 81.

6. Derrida, p. 81.

7. Robert Scholes, *Textual Power* (New Haven: Yale University Press, 1985), p. 21.

8. Scholes, p. 21-22.

9. Scholes, p. 22.

10. Scholes, p. 23.

11. Scholes, p. 24.

12. Virginia Woolf, quoted in Jane Marcus, "Liberty, Sorority, Misogyny" in *The Representation of Women in Fiction*, edited by Carolyn Heilbrun and Margaret Higonnet (Baltimore: Johns Hopkins University Press, 1983), p. 60.

13. Dale Spender, *Man Made Language* (London: Rutledge and Kegan Paul, 1980), p. 12.

14. Stanley Fish, *Is There a Text in This Class?* (Cambridge: Harvard University Press, 1980), p. 243.

15. K.K. Ruthven, *Feminist Literary Studies* (Cambridge: Cambridge University Press, 1984), p. 59.

16. Robert Scholes, *Semiotics and Interpretation* (New Haven: Yale University Press, 1985), p. 127.

17. Jane Gallop, "Snatches of Conversation" in *Women and Language in Literature and Society* (New York: Praeger Publications, 1980), edited by S. McConnell-Ginet, p. 274.

18. Gallop, p. 274.

19. S. McConnell-Ginet, *Women and Language in Literature*, pp. 11-12.

20. Marcus, "Liberty," p. 63.

21. Julia Kristeva, *Desire in Language*, p. 279.

22. Moi, *Sexual*, p. 104.

23. Carol Gilligan, *In a Different Voice* (Cambridge: Harvard University Press, 1982), p. 12.

24. Gilligan, pp. 173-174.

25. Carol Christ, *Diving Deep and Surfacing* (Boston: Beacon Press, 1980), p. 97.

26. Dorothy Richardson, *The Tunnel*, quoted by Rachel Du Plessis in *Writing Beyond the Ending* (Bloomington: Indiana University Press, 1985), p. 145.

27. Jane Austen, *Northhanger Abbey* (Harmondsworth: Penguin, 1972), p. 37.

28. S.M. Gilbert and S. Gubar, *The Madwoman in the Attic* (New Haven: Yale University Press, 1979), p. 34.

29. Kathryn Weibel, *Mirror, Mirror: Images of Women Reflected in Popular Culture* (New York: Anchor Books, 1977), p. 37.

30. Marion Engel, *The Honeyman Festival* (Toronto: Anansi, 1970), p. 130.

31. Arnold Bennett, *On Women*, quoted by Patricia Stubbs in *Women and Fiction* (London: Mcthuen, 1979), p. 204.

32. Annis Pratt, *Archetypal Patterns in Women's Fiction* (Bloomington: Indiana University Press, 1981), p. 135.

33. Stubbs, *Women and Fiction*, p. 235.

34. Ursula LeGuin, *Language of the Night* (New York: Pedigree Books, 1979), p. 169.

35. Engel, *Honeyman*, pp. 1, 2; p. 131.

36. Engel, *Honeyman*, Ibid.

37. Gilbert and Gubar, *Madwoman*, p. 134.

38. Margaret Atwood, *Surfacing* (Toronto: McClelland and Stewart, 1972), p. 191.

39. Scholes, *Textual Power*, p. 165.

40. Scholes, *Textual Power*, p. 165.

41. Northrop Frye, "Expanding the Boundaries of Literature". Unpublished lecture in the *Mind and Matter Series*, Victoria College, 1983.

CHAPTER TWO

1. Virginia Woolf, *A Room of One's Own* (London: Grenada, 1977), pp. 70-71.

2. Mary Poovey, *The Proper Lady and the Woman Writer* (Chicago: University of Chicago Press, 1984), pp. 241-242.

3. W.H. Auden, "Letter to Lord Byrin," in *Collected Longer Poems* (New York: Random House, 1969), p. 41.

4. Jane Austen, *Emma* (Harmondsworth: Penguin, 1985), p. 86.

5. Austen, *Emma*, p. 87.

6. S. M. Gilbert and S. Gubar, *The Madwoman in the Attic* (New Haven: Yale University Press, 1979), p. 113.

7. Austen, *Emma*, p. 62.

8. Austen, *Emma*, p. 63.

9. Rachel Brownstein, *Becoming a Heroine* (New York: Penguin Books, 1984), p. 139.

10. Austen, *Emma*, p. 163.

11. Brownstein, *Heroine*, p. 140.

12. Gilbert and Gubar, *Madwoman*, p. 159.
13. Austen, *Emma*, pp. 418-419.
14. Gilbert and Gubar, *Madwoman*, pp. 159-160.
15. Mary Poovey, *The Proper Lady and the Woman Writer* (Chicago: University of Chicago Press, 1984), p. 237.
16. Erica Jong, *Three Eighteenth Century Novels* (New York: New American Library, 1982), p. vi.
17. Jong, p. vii.
18. Jong, p. vii.
19. B.T. Hunter, *That Scatterbrain Booky* (Toronto: Scholastic-TAB Publications, 1981), p. 74.
20. Hunter, p. 37.
21. Hunter, pp. 28-29.

CHAPTER THREE

1. Thomas Hardy, "We Field Women" in *Landscape Poets: Thomas Hardy* (London: Weidenfeld and Nicholson, 1981), p. 23.
2. Thomas Hardy, *Tess of the D'Urbervilles* (Harmondsworth: Penguin, 1978), p. 137.
3. Michael Riffaterre, "On the Diegetic Function of Description" given at the Fifth International Summer Institute for Semiotic and Structural Studies, June 15, 1984.
4. Hardy, *Tess*, p. 427.
5. Hardy, *Tess*, p. 61.
6. Dorothy van Ghent, *The English Novel: Form and Function* (New York: Harper and Row, 1961), p. 209.
7. Hardy, *Tess*, p. 37.
8. Jeanette King, *Tragedy in the Victorian Novel* (Cambridge: Cambridge University Press, 1978), p. 117.
9. Clive Beck, *Moral Education in the Schools* (Toronto: OISE, 1971), p. 28.
10. Hardy,*Tess*, p. 131.
11. Hardy, p. 150.
12. Hardy, p. 119.
13. Hardy, p. 37.
14. King, *Tragedy*, p. 113.
15. King, p. 114.
16. King, p. 114.
17. Margaret Laurence, *The Diviners* (Toronto: Bantam, 1975), p. 225.

18. Hardy, *Tess*, p. 51.
19. Hardy, p. 99.
20. Hardy, p. 69.
21. van Ghent, *The English Novel*, p. 202.
22. Hardy, *Tess of the D'Urbervilles*, p. 141.
23. Hardy, *Tess*, p. 141.
24. Hardy, pp. 149-150.
25. Hardy, p. 76.
26. King, *Tragedy*, p. 97.
27. King, p. 300.
28. King, p. 313.
29. King, p. 421.
30. King, p. 360.
31. Northrop Frye, *Anatomy of Criticism* (Princeton: Princeton University Press, 1957), pp. 38-39.
32. Hardy, *Tess*, p. 244.
33. King, *Tragedy*, pp. 118-119.
34. Hardy, *Tess*, p. 180.
35. Hardy, p. 238.
36. Hardy, p. 145.
37. Hardy, p. 402.
38. Hardy, p. 231.
39. Hardy, p. 467.
40. King, *Tragedy*, pp. 115-116.
41. Ursula LeGuin, *Language of the Night* (New York: Pedigree Books, 1979), p. 67.
42. Hardy, *Tess*, p. 474.
43. King, *Tragedy*, p. 119.
44. Tillie Olsen, "I Stand Here Ironing" in *Women and Fiction*, edited by Susan Cahill (New York: Mentor Books, 1975), p. 168.
45. Olsen, p. 171.
46. Olsen, p. 171.
47. Doris Lessing, "To Room Nineteen" in *Women and Fiction*, p. 198.
48. Lessing, p. 210.
49. Lessing, p. 209.
50. Lessing, p. 214.
51. Anne Hébert, *Kamouraska* (Toronto: General Publishing, 1982), p.21.

CHAPTER FOUR

1. Cynthia Ozick, "A Master's Mind," in the *New York Times Magazine*, 26 October 1986, p. 29.
2. Terry Eagleton, *Literary Theory* (Oxford: Basil Blackwell, 1983), pp. 189-190.
3. Henry James, *Portrait of a Lady* (London: Macmillan, 1921), vol. 1, p. 60.
4. James, p. 64.
5. James, p. 40.
6. Rachel Brownstein, *Becoming a Heroine* (New York: Penguin Books, 1984), p. 250.
7. G.B. Shaw, *Androcles and the Lion* (Harmondsworth: Penguin, 1951), p. 72.
8. James, *Portrait of a Lady* Vol.1, p. 63.
9. James, p. 57.
10. James, p. 165.
11. James, p. 197.
12. James, p. 202.
13. Brownstein, *Heroine*, p. 262.
14. James, pp. 252-253.
15. James, p. 253.
16. James, *Portrait of a Lady*, Vol. 2, p. 293.
17. James, Vol. 2, p. 48.
18. James, vol. 2, p. 126.
19. F.W. Dupee, *The Question of Henry James: A Collection of Critical Essays* (New York: H. Holt, 1945), p. 121.
20. Fred Millet, *Introduction*, *Portrait of a Lady*, vol. 1, p. xxiii.
21. James, *Portrait of a Lady*, vol. 2, p. 126.
22. James, vol. 2, pp. 171-172.
23. James, vol. 2, p. 70.
24. James, vol. 2, p. 70.
25. James, vol. 2, p. 176.
26. James, vol. 2, p. 168.
27. James, vol. 2, p. 167.
28. James, vol. 2, p. 315.
29. James, vol. 2, p. 343.
30. James, vol. 2, p. 364.
31. James, vol. 2, p. 311.
32. James, vol. 2, pp 311-312.
33. James, vol. 2, p. 368.

34. James, vol. 2, p. 250.
35. Mark Seltzer, *Henry James and the Art of Power* (Ithaca: Cornell University Press, 1984), p. 15.
36. Somerset Maugham, "The Promise" in *Collected Short Stories* (London: Pan, 1975), vol. 1, p. 440.
37. Maugham, p. 440.
38. Maugham, p. 441.
39. Maugham, p. 442.
40. Maugham, pp. 443-444.
41. Brownstein, *Heroine*, p. 276.
42. Virginia Woolf, *To the Lighthouse*, (London: Grenada, 1977).
43. Grace Stewart, *A New Mythos* (Montreal: Eden Press, 1981), p.96.
44. Woolf, *Lighthouse*, p. 21.
45. Stewart, *Mythos*, p. 69.
46. Woolf, *Lighthouse*, p. 107.
47. Woolf, p. 163.
48. Woolf, p. 163.
49. Woolf, p. 114.
50. Carolyn Heilbrun, quoted by Toril Moi in *Sexual Textual Politics* (New York: Methuen, 1985), p. 15.
51. Stewart, *Mythos*, p. 73.
52. Moi, *Sexual*, p. 13.
53. Woolf, *Lighthouse*, p. 163.
54. Lyn Cook, *A Treasure for Tony* (Cobalt: Highway Books, 1980), p.95.
55. Cook, p. 172.
56. Cook, p. 170.

CHAPTER FIVE

1. S. M. Gilbert and S. Gubar, *The Madwoman in the Attic* (New Haven: Yale University Press, 1979), p. xii.
2. Margaret Laurence, *The Diviners* (Toronto: Bantam, 1975), p. 82.
3. Laurence, p. 17.
4. Laurence, p. 62.
5. Laurence, p. 379.
6. Laurence, pp. 33-34.
7. Laurence, p. 87.
8. Laurence, p. 177.
9. Laurence, p. 179.

10. Laurence, p. 165.

11. Laurence, p. 255.

12. Laurence, p. 226.

13. Laurence, p. 248.

14. Laurence, p. 253.

15. Laurence, p. 406.

16. Laurence, p. 295.

17. Elaine Showalter, "Feminist Criticism in the Wilderness" in *Writing and Sexual Difference*, edited by Elizabeth Abel (Chicago: University of Chicago Press, 1982), p. 31.

18. T.S. Eliot, "The Waste Land" in *The Complete Poems and Plays, 1909-1950* (New York: Harcourt, Brace, 1952), p. 49.

19. Margaret Laurence, *The Diviners*, p. 378.

20. Laurence, p. 338.

21. Laurence, p. 329.

22. Laurence, p. 396.

23. Laurence, p. 60.

24. Laurence, p. 450.

25. Claire Mackay, *The Minerva Program* (Toronto: James Lorimer, 1984), p. 94.

26. Mackay, p. 37.

27. Mackay, p. 66-67.

28. Mackay, p. 120.

29. Mackay, p. 116.

30. Mackay, p. 118.

31. Mackay, p. 25.

32. Bruno Bettleheim, *The Uses of Enchantment* (New York: Vintage Books, 1977), p. 164.

33. Bettleheim, p. 161.

34. Bettleheim, p. 166.

35. Elizabeth Janeway, "Meg, Jo, Beth, Amy and Louisa" in *Only Connect*, edited by Sheila Egoff (Toronto: Oxford University Press, 1969), p.287.

36. Janeway, pp. 289-290.

37. Janeway, p. 290.

38. Janeway, p. 290.

39. Louisa Alcott, *Little Women* (London: J.M. Dent, 1975), p. 3.

40. Alcott, p. 31.

41. Alcott, p. 204.

42. Alcott, pp. 262-263.

43. Margaret Mitchell, *Gone With the Wind* (Toronto: Macmillan of Canada, 1936), p. 567.

44. Mitchell, p. 578.
45. Mitchell, p. 183.
46. Mitchell, p. 192-193.
47. Mitchell, pp. 5-6.
48. Mitchell, p. 660.
49. Mitchell, p. 959.
50. Mitchell, p. 948.
51. Mitchell, p. 946.
52. Mitchell, p. 947.

CHAPTER SIX

1. Terry Eagleton, *Literary Theory* (Oxford: Basil Blackwell, 1983), pp. 148-149.
2. Alice Munro, *Who do You Think You Are* (Toronto: MacMillan, 1978), p. 13.
3. Dorothy Dinnerstein, *The Mermaid and the Minotaur* (New York: Harper and Row, 1977), p. 237.
4. Rachel Brownstein, *Becoming a Heroine* (New York: Penguin Books, 1984), p. 35.
5. Munro, p. 28.
6. Munro, p. 26.
7. Munro, p. 31.
8. Munro, p. 32.
9. Munro, p. 24.
10. Munro, pp. 63-64.
11. Munro, p. 44.
12. Munro, p. 45.
13. Munro, p. 45.
14. Wallace Stevens, quoted by Brownstein, p. 239.
15. Munro, p. 71.
16. Charles Kingsley, "A Farewell", stanza 3.
17. Munro, p. 71.
18. Dinnerstein, p. 236.
19. Munro, p. 72.
20. Munro, p. 76.
21. Munro, p. 77.
22. Munro, p. 77.
23. Munro, p. 104.
24. Munro, p. 104.

25. S. McConnell-Ginet, *Women and Language in Literature and Society* (New York: Praeger Publications, 1980), p. 290.

26. Munro, p. 151.

27. Munro, p. 144.

28. Munro, p. 173.

29. Munro, p. 186.

30. Eagleton, p. 191.

31. E.J. Phelps, *Tatterhood and Other Tales* (New York: The Feminist Press, 1978), p. 5. The next five quotations are also from this work.

32. *Tatterhood*, p. 6.

33. Susan Cahill, *Women and Fiction* (New York: Mentor Books, 1975), p.333.

34. Margaret Drabble, in Cahill, pp. 333-334.

35. Margaret Drabble, "The Gifts of War" in Cahill, p. 335.

36. Drabble, p. 336.

37. Drabble, p. 336.

38. Maurice Sendak, *Higglety Pigglety Pop* (New York: Harper and Row, 1967), p. 3.

39. Sendak, p. 5.

40. Northrop Frye, *Divisions on a Ground* (Toronto: Anansi, 1982), p.69.

41. Margaret Atwood, *Surfacing* (Toronto: McClelland and Stewart, 1972), p. 69.

42. Atwood, p. 9.

43. Atwood, p. 17.

44. Atwood, p. 107.

45. Carol Christ, *Diving Deep and Surfacing* (Boston: Beacon Press, 1980), pp. 45-46.

46. Christ, p. 46.

47. Christ, p. 51.

48. Christ, p. 46.

49. Atwood, p. 188.

CONCLUSION

1. Jane Rule, *Lesbian Images* (Trumansburg: The Crossing Press Feminist Series, 1982), preface.

2. Rule, Ibid.

APPENDIX

1. Margaret Atwood, *Second Words: Selected Critical Prose* (Toronto: Anansi, 1982), p. 340.
2. Northrop Frye, *The Stage Is All the World* (Stratford: Stratford Festival, 1985), p. 2.
3. Carol Gilligan, *In a Different Voice* (Cambridge: Harvard University Press, 1982), Chapter 2.
4. Janette Turner Hospital, *Dislocations* (Toronto: McClelland and Stewart, 1986), p. 168.
5. Thomas Kuhn, "The Structure of Scientific Revolutions" in *International Encyclopedia of Unified Science* (Chicago: University of Chicago Press, 1970), vol. 2, p. 10, p. 64.

▲

BIBLIOGRAPHY

Abel, Elizabeth, ed. *Writing and Sexual Difference*. Chicago: University of Chicago Press, 1982.

Aitken, Johan. "Letting Stories Out." Interview with Rudy Wiebe. *Orbit 70*, Vol. 15, No. 2, April 1984.

Alcott, Louisa. *Little Women*. London: J.M. Dent, 1975.

Atwood, Margaret. *Second Words: Selected Critical Prose*. Toronto: Anansi, 1982.

——————. *Surfacing*. Toronto: McClelland and Stewart, 1972.

Auden, W.H. *Collected Longer Poems*. New York: Random House, 1969.

Auerbach, Nina. *Romantic Imprisonment: Women and Other Glorified Outcasts*. New York: Columbia University Press, 1985.

Austen, Jane. *The complete Novels of Jane Austen*. New York: Random House, 1950.

——————. *Emma*. Harmondsworth: Penguin, 1985.

——————. *Northanger Abbey*. Harmondsworth: Penguin, 1972.

——————. *Pride and Prejudice*. Harmondsworth: Penguin, 1972.

Bate, W.J., ed. *Criticism: the Major Texts*. New York: Harcourt, Brace, 1952.

——————. *Criticism: the Major Texts*. New York: Harcourt Brace Jovanovich, 1970.

Beach, J.W. *The Method of Henry James*. New Haven: Yale University Press, 1918.

Beck, Clive. *Ethics*. Toronto: McGraw Hill Ryerson, 1972

——————. *Moral Education in the Schools*. Profiles in Practical Education Series. Toronto: Ontario Institute for Studies in Education, 1971.

Bettleheim, Bruno. *The Uses of Enchantment*. New York: Vintage Books, 1977.

Blackmur, R.P. Introduction to *The Art of the Novel: Critical Prefaces*, by Henry James. New York: Scribner, 1934.

Bloom, Harold. *Deconstruction and Criticism*. New York: Seabury, 1979.

Brownstein, Rachel. *Becoming A Heroine*. New York: Penguin Books, 1984.

Cahill, Susan, ed. *Women and Fiction*. New York: Mentor Books, 1975.

Cargill, Oscar. *The Novels of Henry James*. New York: Macmillan, 1961.

Christ, Carol. *Diving Deep and Surfacing*. Boston: Beacon Press, 1980.

Cook, Lyn. *A Treasure for Tony*. Cobalt: Highway Books, 1980.

Crews, Frederick. *The Tragedy of Manners*. New Haven: Yale University Press, 1957.

Defoe, Daniel. *Moll Flanders*. New York: Modern Library, 1950.

_____. *Moll Flanders* in *Three Eighteenth Century Novels*. Introduction by Erica Jong. New York: New American Library, 1982.

Delaney, Sheila. *Writing Woman*. New York: Schocken Books, 1983.

Dinnerstein, Dorothy. *The Mermaid and the Minotaur*. New York: Harper and Row, 1977.

Donovan, Josephine, ed. *Feminist Literary Criticism*. Lexington: University of Kentucky Press, 1975.

Drabble, Margaret. "The Gifts of War." In *Women and Fiction*, ed. Susan Cahill. New York: Mentor Books, 1975.

_____. *The Needle's Eye*. Harmondsworth: Penguin, 1972.

Dupee, F.W. *The Question of Henry James: A Collection of Critical Essays*. New York: H. Holt, 1945.

Du Plessis, Rachel. *Writing Beyond the Ending*. Bloomington: Indiana University Press, 1985.

Eagleton, Terry. *The Function of Criticism*. Thetford: Thetford Press, 1984.

_____. *Literary Theory*. Oxford: Basil Blackwell, 1983.

Egoff, Sheila. *Only Connect*. Toronto: Oxford University Press, 1969.

Eliot, George. *Middlemarch*. 2 vols. London: J.M. Dent and Sons, 1959.

Eliot, T.S. *The Complete Poems and Plays, 1909-1950*. New York: Harcourt Brace, 1952.

Engel, Marion. *Bear*. Toronto: McClelland and Stewart, 1976.

_____. *The Honeymoon Festival*. Toronto: Anansi, 1970.

Fish, Stanley. *Is There a Text in This Class?* Cambridge: Harvard University Press, 1980.

Fleming, Anne Taylor. "The American Wife" in The *New York Times Magazine*, 26 October 1986, p. 28.

Foucault, Michel. "The Discourse on Language" in *The Archeology of Knowledge and the Discourse on Language*. Trans. A.M. Sheridan Smith. New York: Pantheon, 1982, pp. 215-238.

Fowles, John. *Daniel Martin*. Boston: Little, Brown, 1977.

Fraser, Sylvia. *The Candy Factory*. Toronto: McClelland and Stewart, 1974.

Frye, Northrop. *Anatomy of Criticism*. Princeton: Princeton University Press, 1957.

_____ *The Critical Path*. Bloomington: Indiana University Press, 1973.

_____. *The Stage Is All the World*. Stratford: Stratford Festival, 1985.

_____. *Divisions on a Ground*. Toronto: Anansi, 1982.

_____. "Expanding the Boundaries of Literature," unpublished lecture in the "Mind and Matter" series. Victoria College, 1983.

Frye, Northrop and Aitken, Johan. "There Is Really No Such Thing As Methodology." *Orbit* 70, Vol 1, February 1970.

Gilbert, S.M. and Gubar, S. *The Madwoman in the Attic*. New Haven: Yale University Press, 1979.

Gilligan, Carol. *In a Different Voice*. Cambridge: Harvard University Press, 1982.

Hardy, Barbara. *The Novels of George Eliot*. London: The Athlone Press, 1959.

Hardy, Thomas. "The Field Woman," in *Landscape Poets: Thomas Hardy*. London: Weidenfeld and Nicholson, 1981.

_____. *A Pair of Blue Eyes*. London: Macmillan, 1975.

_____. *Tess of The D'Urbervilles*. Harmondsworth: Penguin, 1978.

Hartman, Geoffrey. *Saving the Text*. Baltimore: John Hopkins University Press, 1981.

Hazard, Shirley. *The Transit of Venus*. New York: Viking Press, 1980.

Hawthorne, Nathaniel. *The Scarlet Letter*. New York: Signet, 1959.

Hébert, Anne. *Kamouraska*. Toronto: General Publishing, 1982.

Heilbrun, Carolyn and Higonnet, Margaret, eds. *The Representation of Women in Fiction*. Baltimore: John Hopkins University Press, 1983.

Heyward, Du Bose. *The Country Bunny*. Boston: Houghton Mifflin, 1939.

Hospital, Janette Turner. *Dislocations*. Toronto: McClelland and Stewart, 1986.

Hunter, B.T. *That Scatterbrain Booky*. Toronto: Scholastic-TAB Publications, 1981.

Inglis, Fred. *The Promise of Happiness*. New York: Cambridge University Press, 1981.

James, Henry. *The Ambassadors*. Introduction by M.W. Sampson and J.C. Gerber. New York: Harper, 1948.

_____. *The Art of the Novel: Critical Prefaces*. New York: Scribner, 1934.

_____. *The Notebooks of Henry James*. Edited by F.O. Mattehiessen and K.B. Murdoch. New York: Oxford University Press, 1947.

_____. *Portrait of a Lady*. 2 vols. London: Macmillan, 1921. (With an introduction by Fred Millet)

Jameson, Fredric. *The Prison House of Language*. Princeton: Princeton University Press, 1972.

Jong, Erica. Introduction to *Three Eighteenth Century Novels*. New York: New American Library, 1982.

Kelley, Mary. *Private Woman, Public Stage*. Oxford: Oxford University Press, 1984.

King, Jeanette. *Tragedy in the Victorian Novel*. Cambridge: Cambridge University Press, 1978.

Kolodny, Annette. "Some Notes on Defining a Feminist Literary Criticism." *Critical Inquiry*, vol. 2 (1975), pp. 75-92.

Kramer, Dale. *Thomas Hardy and the Forms of Tragedy*. Detroit: Wayne State University Press, 1975.

Kristeva, Julia. *Desire in Language: a Semiotic Approach to Literature and Art,* Edited by Leon S. Rondiez, New York: Columbia University Press, 1980.

Krook, Dorothea. *The Ordeal of Consciousness in Henry James*. Cambridge: Cambridge University Press, 1962.

Kuhn, Thomas. "The Structure of Scientific Revelations." In *International Encyclopedia of Unified Science*, 2. Chicago: University of Chicago Press, 1970.

Laurence, Margaret. *The Diviners*. Toronto: Bantam, 1975.

Le Guin, Ursula. *Language of the Night*. New York: Pedigree Books, 1979.

_____. *The Left Hand of Darkness*. New York: Grosset and Dunlap, 1969.

Lessing, Doris. "To Room Nineteen" in *Women and Fiction*. Edited by Susan Cahill. New York: Mentor Books, 1975.

Lewis, C.S. *The Lion, the Witch and the Wardrobe*. London: Collins, 1965.

Lurie, Alison, ed. *Clever Gretchen and Other Forgotten Folktales*. New York: Thomas Y. Crowell, 1980.

Lurie, Alison. *The Language of Clothes*. New York: Random House, 1981.

Mackay, Claire. *The Minerva Program*. Toronto: James Lorimer, 1984.

Marcus, Jane. *New Feminist Essays on Virginia Woolf*. Lincoln: University of Nebraska Press, 1981.

Matthiesses, F.O. *Henry James: The Major Phase*. London: Oxford University Press, 1944.

Maugham, W. Somerset. "The Promise" in *Collected Short Stories*, vol. 1. London: Pan, 1975.

McConnell-Ginet, S. ed. *Women and Language in Literature and Society*. New York: Praeger Publications, 1980.

Meese, Elizabeth. *Crossing the Double Cross*. Chapel Hill: University of North Carolina Press, 1986.

Miller, Jane. *Women Writing About Men*. New York: Pantheon, 1987.

Minard, Rosemary, ed. *Womenfolk and Fairy Tales*. Boston: Houghton Mifflin, 1975.

Mitchell, Margaret. *Gone With the Wind*. Toronto: Macmillan of Canada, 1936.

Moi, Toril. *Sexual Textual Politics*. New York: Methuen, 1985.

Montgomery, L.M. *Anne of Green Gables*. Toronto: McGraw-Hill Ryerson, 1968.

Munro, Alice. *Who Do You Think You Are?* Toronto: Macmillan, 1978.

_____. *The Politics of Love*. Toronto: McClelland and Stewart, 1986.

O'Brien, Mary. *The Politics of Reproduction*. Boston: Routledge & Kegan Paul, 1981.

O'Dell, Scott. *Island of the Blue Dolphin*. Boston: Houghton Mifflin, 1960.

Olsen, Tillie. "I Stand Here Ironing" in *Women and Fiction*. Edited by Susan Cahill. New York: Mentor Books, 1975.

Opie, Iona and Opie, Peter, eds. *The Classic Fairy Tales*. London: Oxford University Press, 1974.

Ozick, Cynthia. "A Master's Mind" in *The New York Times Magazine*, 26 October, 1986, p. 29.

Phelps, E.J., ed. *Tatterhood and Other Tales*. New York: The Feminist Press, 1978.

Pierson, Ruth. *They're Women After All*. Toronto: McClelland and Stewart, 1986.

Poirier, Richard. *The Comic Sense in Henry James*. London: Chatto and Windus, 1960.

Poovey, Mary. *The Proper Lady and the Woman Writer*. Chicago: University of Chicago Press, 1984.

Pratt, Annis. *Archetypal Patterns in Women's Fiction*. Bloomington: Indiana University Press, 1981.

Ray, William. *Literary Meaning: From Phenomenology to Deconstruction*. Oxford: Basil Blackwell, 1984.

Rule, Jane. *Lesbian Images*. Trumansburg: The Crossing Press Feminist Series, 1982.

Ruthven, K.K. *Feminist Literary Studies*. Cambridge: Cambridge University Press, 1984.

Scholes, Percy, ed. *The Oxford Companion to Music*. London: Oxford University Press, 1960.

Scholes, Robert. *Textual Power*. New Haven: Yale University Press, 1985.

———. *Semiotics and Interpretation*. New Haven: Yale University Press, 1985.

Seltzer, Mark. *Henry James and the Art of Power*. Ithaca: Cornell University Press, 1984.

Sendak, Maurice. *Higglety Pigglety Pop!* New York: Harper and Row, 1967.

Shaw, George Bernard. *Androcles and the Lion*. London: Constable, 1951.

Showalter, Elaine. "Feminist Criticism in the Wilderness" in *Writing and Sexual Difference*. Edited by Elizabeth Abel. Chicago: University of Chicago Press, 1982.

Spender, Dale. *Man Made Language*. London: Routledge & Kegan Paul, 1980.

Stewart, Grace. *A New Mythos*. Montreal: Eden Press, 1981.

Stubbs, Patricia. *Women and Fiction*. London: Methuen, 1979.

Sturrock, John. *Structuralism and Since*. Oxford: Oxford University Press, 1979.

Sullivan, Rosemary. *Stories by Canadian Women*. Toronto: Oxford University Press, 1984.

Thomas, D.M. *The White Hotel*. Harmondsworth: Penguin, 1981.

Tolstoy, Leo. *Anna Karenina*. New York: Bantam, 1960.

van Ghent, Dorothy. *The English Novel: Form and Function*. New York: Harper and Row, 1961.

Vetterling-Braggins, Mary, ed. *Sexist Language: A Modern Philosophical Analysis*. Totowa, New Jersey: Littlefield Adams & Co., 1981.

Weibel, Kathryn. *Mirror, Mirror: Images of Women Reflected in Popular Culture*. New York: Anchor Books, 1977.

Welty, Endora. "The Worn Path" in *Women and Fiction*, ed. Susan Cahill. New York: New American Library, 1975.

Woolf, Virginia. *A Room of One's Own*. London: Grenada, 1977.

———. *To The Lighthouse*. London: Grenada, 1977.

Wollstonecroft, Mary. *Vindications of the Rights of Women*. Harmondsworth: Penguin, 1983.

▲

Winner of the Ontario Confederation of University Faculty Associations' Teaching Award, Dr. Johan Aitken is a professor in the School of Graduate Studies at the University of Toronto. Cross-appointed at the Ontario Institute for Studies in Education and the Faculty of Education she has previously authored articles and books of literary criticism.